LIFELINES

Daily Antidotes to Animus and Angst

LIFELINES

Daily Antidotes to Animus and Angst

by Bobbie Wayne

DISCLAIMER

None of the suggested tasks listed in "LIFELINES, Daily Antidotes to Animus and Angst" are to be taken as clinical advice. If you feel seriously upset, anxious, angry or confused, please consult a licensed professional for help.

LIFELINES

Daily Antidotes to Animus and Angst

by Bobbie Wayne

DISCLAIMER

None of the suggested tasks listed in "LIFELINES, Daily Antidotes to Animus and Angst" are to be taken as clinical advice. If you feel seriously upset, anxious, angry or confused, please consult a licensed professional for help.

For Dan, who first found me in Grand Central Station,

and all the other places and times I've been lost.

INTRODUCTION

It began slowly in 2012. I would be awakened at 3 a.m. each morning by a sly, seeping sensation like an icy gel oozing through my veins. As weeks passed, a feeling of dread began to oppress me until I could no longer bear to go to my studio to paint. Staying at home, I found that I couldn't remember how to play my harp; the fingerings just didn't make any sense.

As a professional artist, writer, storyteller, songwriter, and musical performer, I had always been a high-energy person who spent my waking hours creating. Throughout my twenties, I worked in psychiatric facilities as a music therapist. Since I had only a Bachelor of Arts in music, I used my creativity on the job to make up ways to help a great range of disabled individuals. Over the course of seven years working in mental health and disability, I had become familiar with disorders like clinical depression, so I assumed, even all these years later, I would recognize any of the symptoms in myself. Yet, I was neither depressed, nor lethargic. Thinking my problems had a physical cause, I spent a year seeing specialists and having tests performed to no avail.

Finally, a clinical psychiatrist correctly diagnosed me as having an anxiety disorder. My brain's "fight-or-flight" switch was malfunctioning, flooding my body with cortisol and adrenaline inappropriately. It took several years of trial and error to find the correct combination of medications to correct my imbalance. Speaking with a social worker helped me identify my "triggers"— those situations most likely to cause an anxiety attack.

My greatest trigger, I found, was feeling helpless. Worries about medical issues, the climate crisis, politics, struggling with technology, and the isolation from working in the arts were all likely to trigger an anxiety attack. I needed to be my own healer and create small, doable daily tasks that would interest and empower me.

As an only child, I spent a great deal of time alone or with one artistic or musical friend making things. Every day was exciting because there were worlds, not just to discover, but to create! To help relieve my symptoms, I decided to give myself a daily assignment of activities, much as I had done in childhood: things like teaching a child to whistle, asking older persons to talk about "what it was like when they were young," getting animal lovers involved in protecting habitat, creating treasure hunts, discovering ways to interact with and learn about people from other cultures and backgrounds and finding ways to understand and help change trends in our government and society that seemed harmful. This turned out to be, along with the correct medication and professional help, exactly what I needed in order to heal.

Four years later, America's political upheaval proved to be challenging to anyone with an anxiety disorder. I realized that others might profit from these assignments as well, so I made sure each was doable by anyone. I continued writing daily assignments for a year, sharing them online with friends. Many people suggested I compile them into a book.

For those who are struggling with family issues, the news, pandemics, or overly programmed lives, doing these tasks may help, and you might possibly make the little piece of the earth you inhabit a bit better, one lifeline at a time. With each page, you will learn to pay closer attention to your senses, environment, community, the world and the perceptions and feelings of others. The tasks employ art, crafts, philosophy, music, socialization, and history, while improving society and the world. They get people laughing again with each other (The book even teaches a tap step to do when you are stuck waiting in a line!)

It is my hope that the tasks in *Lifelines* will be shared within families, at the office, and on the internet, where they will spread like beneficial seeds in what has become a barren landscape. All these tasks are made to share with others, so "pass it on!" It's what kids whisper to each other when they pass notes. This book is my note—of hope. Please, pass it on.

CREDO

Look up a dictionary definition of the word "credo." Spend a week thinking about your own personal statement. Jot down notes. Try to distill your notes into one concise statement. Once you have written your credo, put it in a safe place.

When you face difficult decisions, pull out your statement to guide you. From time to time, review your credo, revising if it's no longer your truth.

ESSENTIAL WATER

Collect rainwater in a bucket that can hold at least a gallon. Once the rain has stopped, use the water immediately in your garden to water your plants, or cover the container since mosquitos will breed in still water. With parental permission, get some neighborhood kids involved. Have them each provide their own containers if they can, or you can collect containers to share with them.

Decide on a period of time throughout which the kids will collect and measure rainfall for their area. After the rain has ceased, the group can measure how much water they each collected and report it. Considering this "data" together, look up areas of the planet suffering from drought and learn about the effects this has upon its inhabitants, human and nonhuman alike. Ask the kids to share what they think about water as an essential need. Ask them to work individually or collaboratively to design a system for saving water instead of wasting it.

COLORS OF THE DAY

Make a diary of sunrises. You will need a small sketchbook. I like the spiral-bound kind because you can open them flat. You'll also need an assortment of pastel pencils. Some art stores sell good selections online, but I prefer going to the store and picking them out myself. Choose a range of blues, greens, reds, violets, and yellows, both dark and light. You'll need a handheld sharpener too.

Each morning, take in the sunrise (to protect your eyes, be careful not to look directly at the sun for too long at any given moment). Determine what colors you see and lightly begin making lines of color in your book. You can use a clean tissue to spread the color over an area. At first, don't bother drawing cloud shapes; just concentrate on laying down the colors as you see them.

You may experiment with lightly layering one color over another. Use only one side of each paper to avoid smudging. You should spray them with fixative (available in arts and crafts stores) to prevent smearing. Do one at the same time each morning and date them. You will be surprised when you look back at your work after several months.

ESTABLISHING BALANCE

These days, we have to carry a lot of belongings around as we go about our day. People who carry all the traditional items in their pockets or a purse, such as a comb, wallet, and car keys, often now have the additional weight of a smartphone, a tablet, or an iPad. In order to prevent neck and back injuries, consider splurging on a small, well-made backpack with a pocket for your computer or device that holds it flat against your back. The straps should be padded and comfortable and should not cut you in the neck or trapezius muscles.

Make sure the pack has a good number of zippered side pockets for staying organized and holding your keys, phones, or change. You do not want everything to sag in the middle of the pack like a rock. That puts pressure on your shoulders. Another helpful strategy is to buy a pack with a light color inside, so you can easily see the small items in the pockets.

You need to be able to stand and walk comfortably while wearing your new pack without thrusting your neck out ahead of your body. So many of us sit this way at our computers, like turtles peering out of our shells. Standing up and carrying ourselves and our belongings from place to place should be restorative.

REST AND REFLECTION

Run away from home for a day. If people (or animals) are dependent upon you, arrange for someone to step in to help. Go for an entire day. Eat your meals somewhere you are not likely to be known. Pack food for yourself if you wish. Take a small notebook with you.

Once you've escaped your life for the day and reached a destination of choice, picture yourself at age six. Spend an hour or two exploring your surroundings, looking at everything through your six-year-old eyes. Write down in your notebook the things you notice. What excites you, frightens you, or makes you sad?

Next, spend some time as your 18-year-old self. Ask yourself similar questions. Journal some more. By now it is likely around midday. Have your lunch pretending to be your 25-year-old self. What do you think of the people you observe around you at the restaurant or outdoor lunch spot? As you savor your food, consider: what would you like the rest of your life to be like?

Plan your afternoon so that you go somewhere new and do something as your 40-year-old self. This time, take a moment to reflect upon the people you have in your life at home. Would they make your 40-year-old self happy? You may divide the late afternoon up as you wish and your age permits. Have dinner out as well, and consider: Are you happy with the life you have made and the people in it? Are there changes you would like to make? Now, when you feel it's time, go back to your life.

ALL THE THINGS YOU ARE

Write a letter to someone who is still alive, in which you tell them all the things you would wish to have said if they suddenly disappeared. Put the letter in a safe place with your important papers: your will, marriage license, your birth certificate.

Update the letter quarterly and replace it with a new one. Indicate on the envelope who should receive it if you die. In the letter, you may wish to say how much and why you love the recipient, how grateful you are for their love, and anything else you would want them to know.

Now, since you are both still alive, make sure you say those things often, even if life has become crowded and busy.

WITH ONE ANOTHER

Consider the word "compassion." This word (originally in Latin 'compassion') is defined by *Britannica Dictionary* as "a feeling of wanting to help someone who is sick, hungry, [or] in trouble . . ." Literally, it means, "to suffer together." But it is more than just an empathetic feeling; compassion involves both recognizing the suffering of others and taking action to alleviate it.

We can rise above a "might makes right" attitude and do the hard work where each of us steps up to try every day to cultivate a community that is fair, just, and caring. Today, ask yourself, "What can I do to be compassionate toward someone?" Then, do it. This may involve helping someone carry a heavy load, defending someone against bullying, or reading proposed legislative bills and expressing your opinion to your local representative.

There are different ways that we "suffer together." Without empathy, we suffer together in the long run, getting the culture we deserve in the end. In compassion, we experience empathy as we strive to rectify the issues and challenges we face.

GET IT DOWN

Join a writing group or form one of your own. The idea is to get together with a group of people once a week and learn how to tell a story on paper. Everyone has a story; many stories, actually. You may want to preserve family tales, or you might be someone who comes up with wonderful ideas for storytelling or screenplays.

Perhaps you want to tell a true story or write an essay about current events. Getting feedback from a group of people can be very helpful. Make sure you establish some ground rules regarding critiquing and the amount of time each person gets to read. If you join an existing group, find out in advance if the writers topics are compatible with your interests. If you write children's stories, you don't want to join a group that writes political satire. Do you want hard critiques or positive feedback? If you are a beginner, you may want gentle feedback until you are more polished. Everyone has, at some time, wanted to write something. Now's your chance!

SEEKING LOVELY MISFITS

Turn off your phone. Go outside and hunt for a four-leaf clover. City parks have them, as well as suburban lawns and country fields. Your quest may take as long as you wish. Bring something good to eat and/or drink.

As you search, pay close attention to the colors of your surroundings, the way the air smells, and the sounds you hear. Close your eyes and feel the grass and weeds and dirt with your hands or bare feet wherever you are seeking your clover. If you don't find the clover this time, you may try again in a new spot. You can even choose to bring a friend or family member along the next time.

If you find a clover, take it home and press it in a book where it will surprise you or someone years later. Should you fail to find a clover, remember, the quest is the important part.

TEACH YOUR FAMILY WELL

Listen to the lyrics of the Rodgers and Hammerstein song "You've Got to be Carefully Taught" from the musical *South Pacific*. We have grown used to seeing dreadful images online and on TV: images of violence, intolerance, and hate. Think about what violent news stories are teaching all of us, especially our kids. Sit down with your family and go around the table discussing everyone's reactions to these news items.

Ask your children what they think. Are they frightened or confused? Make a family plan to deal with these upsetting stories. Empower your children and yourselves. Do not let the news, social media, TV, friends, the radio, or the papers go unchallenged.

Help everyone to write letters to elected officials to protest hate crimes. Show people how to fact-check their sources of news. Teach them to be on the side of the good. Remember, "You've got to be carefully taught."

SHALL WE DANCE?

Learn a simple tap step: the Shuffle Stamp and use it to perform a tap "combination."

1. Stand with weight on both feet.

2. Shift your weight to your left leg and pick up your right knee.

3. Swing your leg forward, glancing the floor in a light tap with the ball of your foot, while continuing your upward motion. Keep your weight on your left leg.

4. Without putting your right leg down, swing it backwards, tapping the ball of your foot as it swings back.

5. Then stamp the right foot lightly next to your left foot. You have just done a Shuffle Step.

6. Now, practice this with the same leg while saying, "shuf-ful stamp," with "shuf" as your leg swings forward, "ful" as it swings backward and "stamp" as you stamp your right foot.

7. Shift your weight onto your right leg and pick up your left knee. Repeat steps 3, 4 and 5 with the left leg, again saying, "shuf-ful-stamp."

8. Now, shift your weight back to your left leg, pick up your right leg once again and repeat steps 3, 4 and 5.

9. Lastly, stamp with the left foot, followed by the right. while saying, "stamp, stamp." The whole combination should sound like this: "Shuf-ful **stamp**, shuf-ful **stamp**, shuf-fle **stamp**, **stamp**, **stamp**." You will end the combination with your weight on your right leg.

Hint: When you stamp, sink down a little by bending both knees. Practice this until you can do it without trouble. Keep your body relaxed; don't stamp hard.

FEAR OF SPEAKING WITH STRANGERS

In recent times, Americans have become fearful of speaking with strangers. Communication between people requires trust. Retreating into one's own comfort zone only separates us, deepening misunderstandings. In order to stem the tide of alienation and loneliness that has swept over our country, we need to talk with each other, regardless of the risks.

If you are stuck in a crowd, such as in an airport, make a little joke, like saying, "Are we all having fun yet?" as you turn and smile at someone next to you who doesn't look like you. Or make it a habit to speak with strangers when you are waiting on a line. If they smile and respond, you can have a little chat. People have much more in common than they think.

Some of us are simply afraid of people unlike ourselves. Others worry that they will be rebuffed for committing unintended micro-aggressions. This is one of the many negative results of poor leadership and inadequate education. Certain politicians, hate groups and some religious organizations have stoked the fires of racism and cultural bigotry, which has led to a rise in mutual mistrust.

Groups that have suffered abuse are, understandably, suspicious of strangers questioning them about their culture, language, dress, hairstyles, etc. If you are part of the abused group, you can be an ambassador by speaking up if someone insults or offends you.

You don't have to explain your culture to rude or clueless people. But sometimes, even well-meaning people make mistakes and offend. This is when pointing out the problem and educating them is helpful to everyone. If *you* find that you have hurt or offended someone, apologize sincerely. Once we establish trust, we can begin to have conversations. Exchanging information is one of the things that makes us human.

RESOLUTION OF AN INJURY

Recall an injury done to you by another person, either recently or in the past. The injury may be slight or great. It may be intentional or not. The perpetrator of the injury may be a stranger, an acquaintance, or someone close to you.

On a small piece of paper, compose one sentence describing the injury as concisely as you can. Work hard on this sentence, trimming away all but the exact injury. On the same paper, write a second sentence stating the essence of how this harmed you. Boil down all the details into this statement. You now have two sentences that should sum up your experience:

     1. This is what was done to me by . . .

     2. What this did to me was . . .

Walk outside with the paper and a sturdy spoon or garden trowel. Find a safe spot where you are alone and unobserved. Dig a little hole at least several inches deep and bury the paper, covering it carefully.

You have symbolically removed this injury from your mind. Tell yourself, "While I may remember the incident, it does not have to determine my future."

THE COLORS OF OUR EYES

Close your eyes and picture the color of your irises. Now look in a mirror at your eyes in the daylight. You may need to take a mirror outside. Look first at the tissues in your irises. Note the color of the deepest layer. See what colors are in the layers atop this.

Note any color change in the area nearest the pupil. Do you have a ring of separate color or deeper value at the outside of each iris where it meets the white of the eyeball? Lastly, see if you have any spots of color that differ from the general color of your irises.

Close your eyes again and try to describe the eye colors of five people you know.

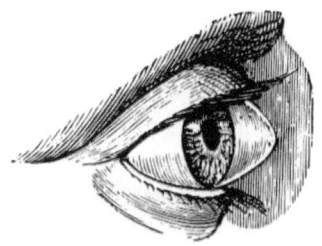

THE GIFT OF READING ALOUD

When you were very young, did someone read to you? One of the greatest ways to encourage a child to read is to read aloud to them. This is a wonderful pleasure for the adult as well. My mother read me *Alice in Wonderland* and *Treasure Island* when I was a pre-schooler. She also read me *Andersen's Fairy Tales* and *Grimms' Fairy Tales*, leaving out the parts that she thought were too mature for me. Naturally, I found each page she omitted on my own and read it, broadening my knowledge.

Your task is to find someone to read to. This does not have to be a young person. People of all ages love having someone read to them. There may be elders in assisted living who don't have any family to come and visit them. Consider volunteering to read to them once a month.

Reading to adolescents can improve their lives as well. Many kids don't read well because they haven't been exposed to books when they were young. Volunteering to tutor in reading skills after school is a great way to get involved. Remember, the material must hold the person's interest. If you can discover what a person is passionate about, you can provide the key to worlds that were formerly unknown.

Graphic novels are available these days which may be an interesting tool for engaging readers who are just beginning to read as adults. Even comic books can be good sources of vocabulary. As a girl, I read every comic book that had to do with horses. Since many took place in the west and southwest, I picked up Spanish words like "mesa," "plateau," "corral" and "canyon."

Once you gain a person's respect and trust, you can ask them if they would enjoy reading aloud to you. Once a person has the skill to fluently read aloud, encourage them to read to someone else.

WHO I AM NOT

On a piece of nice paper, print or write neatly the words, "I AM NOT MY PAST." Hang it where you will see it frequently throughout the day. Go on from there.

A CHILD'S VIEW OF HOLIDAYS

Ask a child whose parents have ok'ed it to tell you the story of the origins of a holiday they celebrate. Don't let the adults around you interrupt. If the child doesn't celebrate any holidays, ask what holiday they would create if they could make up any holiday in the world. Prepare to be surprised! It could be something as silly as "Peanut Butter and Jelly Day." Or as solemn as "I Miss My Old Dog Day."

Marking important aspects of our lives gives us something to look forward to. Holidays are occasions that draw families and friends together, reminding us of commonly held beliefs, creating new memories. Festive foods, special music, and ceremonies preserve and extend our cultures.

Children are introduced to their particular group's customs and beliefs through stories and special events. Explaining their holiday's origins is fun for the young person themself, as well as the older members of the gathering, some of whom may recall their own youthful traditions.

A SOURCE BOOK FOR SONGS

Purchase an inexpensive blank journal, with or without lines. On the first page of this "song journal," list ten simple tunes you can easily hear in your mind. They may be nursery rhymes or folk songs or even favorite rock songs from your teen years.

Carry your journal with you during the day. Notice when you are experiencing a particular mood, and jot down words or phrases that describe your feelings. Take the time, then or later, to draft a little poem using some of the ideas or words you wrote. Shape the poem so that it fits the rhythm of one of the songs on your list. It doesn't have to rhyme. Write out a more final draft neatly in your journal. Do this for a month or more, adding more complicated songs if you wish.

YOUR LISTENING SELF

Go outside with a beach towel or blanket. Find a place where you can lie down on the ground. This can be in a field, in a park, in a yard, on a beach, or any place where you can touch the earth. Make sure you will be warm enough. Spread the towel/blanket on the ground and lie on your back. Close your eyes. Notice when you begin to breathe normally.

Now listen, noting any human-made sounds, known as the anthropophony, including noise from airplanes. Next, listen to the earth (the geophony): Is the wind blowing through the grass, trees, or across the water? Now, can you hear the sounds of insects, animals, or birds (the biophony)?

Inhale deeply, noting the different odors around you. Describe these scents to yourself. Still with your eyes closed, stretch out your arms and legs. Attempt to feel the planet's curving surface. Enjoy the solidity of the earth supporting you.

UNLOCKING MINDS

Find a key you no longer use. Securely attach to it a small note written on heavy paper (or possibly an index card) which reads, "You are the key to your own future." Leave the key in a public place where a teenager is likely to find it, such as a bench outside a high school or a coffee house frequented by young people.

WE'RE ALL FROM SOMEWHERE

Ask relatives if they are willing to discuss your family's heritage. If so, write down when each branch of your family arrived in this country. How did they get here? Where did they settle? What jobs did they take?

Now go online and look up the races, religions, and nationalities of the people who were already here when your ancestors arrived. What were their similarities to your people? What were their differences? How were your ancestors welcomed or rejected by those who lived here? Lastly, how do you and your family feel about people newly immigrating today?

TO ACT AND WHEN

"Let sleeping dogs lie" is an expression anyone with a new puppy can appreciate. Puppy training can be exhausting work; however, it's essential to correct bad habits before they become serious problems. Once the puppy is sleeping, most family members are grateful for a break. "Let sleeping dogs lie," they tell anyone in the room. But really, this expression is a euphemism for not disturbing the status quo.

Why not address small problems before they grow into large ones? Think of a task you have been reluctant to face. In one sentence, put the task into words. Next, list the things preventing you from dealing with it. Work on solving these things, one by one. Let's say, for example, you have had intermittent tooth pain that you have been ignoring for a month. There are three things preventing you from dealing with it:

1. You can't seem to remember to make your yearly dental appointment.

2. You might have to take a day off from work.

3. You are afraid the dentist will order a root canal.

Instead of telling yourself that the pain isn't really that bad since you only feel it at times, place a note on your bathroom mirror reminding you to make an appointment. Ask the dentist if you can see her late in the afternoon or early morning. Decide that you will not worry about the cause of the pain because worrying won't help. Congratulate yourself for taking action.

SHARE THE STEP

Have you learned the tap combination on page number 12? Here's where you get to use it! In your travels, when you are waiting around somewhere with a bunch of strangers, do your tap combination. Choose an unobstructed roomy place without a carpet, such as a train station, a garden center or an area where you won't interfere with the flow of traffic.

Your goal is to amuse and engage people without disturbing others. Hospitals, places of worship and libraries are, therefore, not good choices. When you start tapping, people may turn and stare. Repeat the combination several times. If people have begun to smile, invite someone in the crowd who looks to be in shape to join you, saying, "Come on, I'll show you. It's easy!" If you persist, someone may eventually try it with you. Have them stand behind you while you show them (it's easier to learn this way). See how many people you can teach. You may be the most memorable and happy thing in someone's day. Making people happy is one of the greatest gifts we can share.

A LITTLE HELP FOR OUR FRIENDS

Buy or gather the seeds of some flowers that are indigenous and helpful to your area. In my neck of the woods, native milkweed and echinacea nourish monarch butterflies and birds. The next time you are out for a walk or a drive, carry the seeds with you in a small container. In addition, bring a couple of full water bottles.

Upon finding an abandoned lot or a weedy, unloved area by the road, stop and scrape up a little dirt in order to plant some of your seeds. If it's an urban area or busy highway, be sure to keep safely away from traffic. Pour the water you brought over the newly planted seeds.

AN UNCOMFORTABLE TRUTH

Learn the lyrics to "Over the River and Through the Woods," or at least print out a bunch of lyric sheets. Pass them out when your guests arrive for Thanksgiving dinner and go around the room, after dinner, each person singing a couplet. If they can't sing, let them speak it. Challenge everyone to write part of a new verse to the tune, updating the lyrics to the present day and your particular family gathering.

Be mindful of the fact that Thanksgiving is a day of sorrow for Native Americans. Look up the history of the first Puritan settlement in Massachusetts and note the behavior of the English newcomers and that of the original inhabitants. Nathaniel Philbrick's book *Mayflower* describes what actually took place upon the European's arrival and in the years that followed. In order to participate fully, all Americans need to understand our country's history; the good and the bad. If native people once inhabited the area in which you live, you may wish to find out who they were, what their culture was like and if their people still exist. Being thankful for our own bounty is more meaningful once we recognize past wrongs and act to right them.

IN DAYS GONE BY

Choose a person you know who is considerably older than you. This can be a relative, a colleague at work, or someone you know socially. Ask this person if they would be willing to share a story with you about what life was like when they were young. If they agree, suggest meeting for tea or coffee in a quiet location. You might even offer to treat!

Listen to the way they tell their story. Pay attention without interrupting. After they finish, pose any questions you have. Most people are honored to give you this gift.

THE LIONHEARTED

The word "courage" comes from Middle English and 12th century French, "corage," with a Latin root "cor" or "cuer," referring to the heart. *Merriam-Webster* defines courage as "the mental or moral strength to venture, persevere, and withstand danger, fear, or difficulty." The *Oxford English Dictionary* says courage is "the ability to do something that frightens one; strength in the face of pain or grief."

Notice that the word "strength" is used in defining courage. The heart is often considered to be the origin of our courage, our spirit, and our strength. Grab your journal and list five to ten sources of your own strength. For example, many people attribute their courage to God. Others may credit their partner, family, or friends. Some may say their workouts or yoga practice provide strength, others, their diet. Some cite their jobs or livelihood. We speak of having "a good heart" or being "young at heart." We call durable or sustaining things "hearty," and counsel people facing disaster to "take heart." I have seen supposedly strong men and women fail to do the right thing because it involved risk, danger, or trouble, while less strong but good-hearted people put themselves and their welfare second to save or help someone.

Are you a person of "corage," or heart? Next, make a list of ten contemporary world leaders. Do they have courage or not? Why do you say that? What examples can you give and where did you find them?

YOUR CLAY IMAGE

At an arts and crafts store, buy a small tub or pack of non-drying modeling clay that is close to your skin tone. You will also need a plastic knife and a toothpick. When you get home, clear a flat space on a counter or desk and cover it with wax paper or parchment. Now you will create a human sculpture out of your clay.

1. Roll a piece of clay about the size of a cherry between your hands and shape it into a small ball.

2. Shape another piece of the clay into a rectangle that is 2 inches by 1 inch, and ½ inch thick.

3. Now, roll a tube of clay 4 ½ inches long and ¼ inch thick. Using the plastic knife, cut a ¼ inch piece from the end of the tube for the neck. Hold the clay rectangle vertically and use your toothpick to work a small hole into the top large enough for one end of the neck. Insert one end of the ½ inch neck piece and work the clay so that the two pieces mold together.

4. The next step is to make a shallow hole in the ball with the toothpick and then insert the other end of the neck piece into it, molding the two pieces together. You have now attached the figurine's head, neck, and torso.

5. Return to the roll from which you cut the neck piece and cut the remaining tube in half. You should have two pieces that are 2 inches long. These will be your arms.

6. Poke holes on each side of the rectangle and attach an arm on each side. Slightly squeeze ⅜ of an inch at the bottom of each arm to form hands.

7. Now make a roll of clay 6 ½ inches long and ⅜ inch wide. Cut the roll in half. These pieces will be the legs.

8. Poke two leg holes at the bottom of the rectangle near the corners. Join each leg to the torso. Bend each leg piece at ½ inch from the bottom at right angles and squeeze slightly to make the feet.

9. Add or remove clay to create the desired shape of your chest and tummy if you wish.

Each day, address your clay image with a greeting and adjust its posture to express your mood. In your travels, observe other people's postures. What would their clay models look like?

MODEL THE GOOD ACTIONS

Remove a shopping cart someone else left blocking a parking spot and wheel it back to where it belongs at the store entrance. Others may see you doing this act of kindness and copy your behavior.

The next person to pull into this empty space will find greater ease of parking and this will help them to have a better day.

FACE THAT REPAIR

Fix something you have been avoiding repairing. Estimate how long the repair will take. Assemble all the tools you will need ahead. If you must buy tools or supplies, break up the task into two days.

Plan ahead before you begin, making sure you have everything you need, including instructions if you don't know exactly how to proceed. Learn which tasks are feasible home repairs and which should be left to a professional. Ask yourself how much your time is worth. If you spend a whole day trying to fix the hole in your screen and ended up cutting yourself, returning to the hardware store several times, having a fight with your family because you broke the door frame, it might be less costly to hire someone to do the repair.

Certain repairs, such as electrical, plumbing, tree and roof work can cause great personal injury without proper training and equipment. Hire a professional for those jobs. This will allow you more time to fix the jobs that have been piling up and distressing you.

RELAX

Choose some quiet instrumental music. At some point in the day or evening, find a place where you can be alone with the music for fifteen minutes. This may be in your car, in a crowd (wear earbuds or headphones) outside, in your bathroom, or wherever you need to go to be undisturbed.

Choose music that is soothing, not stimulating. Close your eyes and think of a happy memory. Take six slow deep breaths, releasing each leisurely. This is your immune-system tune-up.

HAPPINESS LIST

In your journal, write "Happiness List" at the top of the page. Then write today's date on the first line at the left-hand margin. Below that, list the dates for the next seven days. You might want to skip a line below each date to give you more room to write. Now, think of one or more things that you can do to make yourself happy for each of the coming seven days. Write them down and make sure to do them.

You can start small if you wish. For example, you may choose to have a favorite dish for supper or begin reading something you've always wanted to read. You might call someone you love talking with. If you have family, you may involve them. You might plan day trips which will turn you into treasure hunters, looking every day for new and exciting things to learn and do.

By planning for and doing something interesting, fun, or uplifting each day, we can defeat boredom and stagnation. We have the power to lighten our moods.

INFANT GRATIFICATION

Don't let the marketers train you to buy things you don't need. In teaching very young children, we often have to get them excited about objects in which they have no interest. The more excited we become, the more the child wants it, especially if we withhold it for a bit. Companies that, for a fee, give people access to purchasing ahead of others use the same techniques: create a need that was not there and fill it to get what *they* want.

This week, start making an inventory of your life. Take note of your basic possessions, furniture, kitchenware, bed, clothing, toys, techy stuff. Ask yourself if there were an emergency and you had to choose ten of your objects to save, which would you keep? Then think about whether or not you are happy in life. Does your stuff make you happy? Finally, rather than griping about how much money billionaires truly need, ask yourself if *you* really need to pay those fees for the privilege of getting to buy more *stuff* faster. Where else could this money be better used? Are you willing to go on being trained like an infant?

AVIAN SPECIES

Watch the birds in your area. Go on a walk and carry something whereby you can note the characteristics of unfamiliar birds. You may think that all you have in your town are sparrows or pigeons, but that isn't the case. Even cities have grassy areas or ponds or rivers where birds can gather or rest along a migration route. Look up your native birds, so you will know how to spot them. Note the difference in their wings; some are short and chop the air in flight, helping them escape predators by flying in-between dense growth, and others are long for gliding.

What kind of bird would you most want to be if you turned into one? Learn all you can about your bird of choice and what they require to thrive. Any activity that draws us outside, into the natural world, takes us away from our worries as we fill our lungs with fresh air. Take your binoculars with you so you can see the birds up close.

SHARING OUR HISTORY

Buy a pocket-sized copy of the Constitution with the Declaration of Independence included. Spend some time learning about our government so that you will be able to speak intelligently about it to others. Put together a reading or discussion group with your family, friends, or coworkers. Have everyone find out something about the topic to share, if possible. Ken Burns' documentary *The Civil War*, with its evocative photos of real people, documents and locations where battles took place, shows us that history is alive. Lin-Manuel Miranda's musical *Hamilton* introduces history to the imaginations of twenty-first century kids and adults, engaging some of us who may have cared nothing about America's past or its government. Get kids and adults interested; challenge them to write their own raps, songs, poems, or plays using something or someone from the Constitution or the Declaration. Let's make America smart again, beginning with ourselves.

BULLIED

In your daily travels, is there someone you often see who doesn't seem to fit in? Kids or adults who are perceived as vulnerable, quiet, or shy are sometimes targeted by bullies. To an extent, this targeting behavior extends into adulthood. If you have ever been bullied, or someone you love has, you know how bad it can make a person feel. This can result in the person becoming withdrawn and fearful.

If you know of someone who gets picked on, made fun of, or left out in your community (at your school, your job, or wherever you happen to be fairly regularly), pay attention to them. They may be victims of trauma. Take a moment out of your busy day to ask them a friendly question or start a conversation. Share something with them; say, "I'm going for coffee. Can I get you some?" If you are young or old and attend any level of school, you might ask this person to sit with you at lunch. Be prepared to graciously accept a refusal, especially if the person is shy.

FIRST AID

Clean out your medicine cabinet. Turn in old drugs at a police station or drugstore and throw away expired over-the-counter drugs. Many police departments now accept expired or unwanted prescription drugs for safe disposal. Make sure you have band-aids of all sizes, peroxide, antibacterial ointment, burn ointment, gauze pads, several widths of Ace bandages and a fully assembled first-aid kit where everyone can find it.

Keep a supply of antacids, and an anti-diarrheal, on hand, as well as aspirin and Ibuprofen. Lock all your drugs away from children. Post the emergency numbers of poison control, your local hospital, and your doctor inside the door of the medicine cabinet where everyone can see it.

If you have pets who take medications, keep their meds in a separate area, locked and well-marked, along with your vet's number. When accidents happen, you don't have time to go running around looking for gauze or scissors. Organizing your medicines and first-aid supplies will pay off.

HOMEMADE CARDS

Cut out pictures from a magazine or newspaper. Look for photos, statements, and artwork that relate to your world or the world of your friends and relatives. To organize your pictures, get a pack of manila envelopes and label one for each individual group such as men, women, kids, furniture, animals, flowers, trees, sayings, and so on.

You may glue them down to make a picture or an abstract design. Then get some blank cards and envelopes at an arts or stationery store. The next time someone's birthday, wedding, or graduation comes around, make your own personalized card with your cut images. For inspiration, look at the collages made by Picasso and Braque, as well as the abstract artists of the '50s and '60s. You can even stick a small object to the card (the flatter, the better) like safety pins, small rings, a tiny rolled-up scroll tied in the middle with a thread, a religious charm, a sticker or a lock of hair tied with a ribbon.

Using tracing paper and a pencil, you can also trace the outlines of things in your cut-out photos. Then you can cut the tracing paper just outside of your traced line and glue it to the collage, going over the tracing with magic markers. For example, you could trace several separate photos of cows and make them outrageous colors, like purple-striped or orange polka dots. The point is to make something original and handmade for the people you love. They will be pleased that you took the time and put thought into their card rather than just buying one at the store.

REMEMBRANCE

Go somewhere quiet with a birthday candle, votive, or other small candle and a candle holder that is safe. Or, if you have a fireplace, you can start a pleasant fire and use that instead of a candle. Make a list of several people who have passed on who had positive influences on you.

Light the candle. While your flame burns, picture each of these people one by one, remembering how they spoke, dressed, and moved. Thank each person that you are remembering for the positive impact they had on your life.

BALANCE

Barefoot, stand on one foot for as long as you can without putting down your other foot. If you can't do it at all, hold the wall or an arm of the sofa, letting go as you acquire balance. Then switch feet. Do this whenever you have downtime and find yourself bored or alone. Increase your time until you feel that you are improving.

Next, as you balance on one foot try moving your other leg around in a small circle or swinging it back and forth. On your standing leg, spin your body in a 360-degree circle (you may have to hop a bit). Once you are able to do all of the above barefoot, try the same in a pair of thin-soled shoes, such as ballet shoes or any flat shoes without heels or thick soles. Take your time with this; your achilles tendon needs to relax if it is not used to being fully extended. It may take weeks or months for your body to coordinate. Our shoes often prevent our foot muscles from working properly, since we can't feel the ground. Many of us are not used to having our heels level with the balls of our feet, especially those of us who spend time wearing high heels. Once you are comfortable balancing without your regular street shoes (such as sneakers, loafers, or the like), put them on and try doing the same exercises.

Next, practice walking on a wide plank laid flat on the ground. Go slowly at first, one foot in front of the other, until you feel totally secure. Take as long as you need to acquire good balance. Once you are confident, the next time you are stuck in a line somewhere or at a social gathering, challenge kids around you to a "stand on one foot" or "walk the plank" contest. When adults scoff at you, challenge them to try it.

STANDING TOGETHER

What does the word "witness" mean to you? Invite some well-meaning, nonviolent people that you know to stand witness with you against hate groups. Our country, from its founding, has been disrupted and plagued by groups whose purpose is to sow discord and mistrust between people. There has been a surge in demonstrations by these hate groups in the last decade, which has resulted in the loss of innocent lives.

All Americans have the right to gather and march in public. The KKK, Neo-Nazis, and other associations that promote hate, odious and destructive as they are, still have the right to free speech, which includes marching through our streets. We, however, have the right to stand witness when we disagree. One way of safely doing this is to organize a peaceful counter-demonstration. Obtain a permit clearing the date, time and place with your local authorities. Make sure that there will be security for your demonstration. Have people within your group call the local news media to notify and invite the public. Determine the goal of your protest so that you can state it clearly. For example, your goal might be to make the community aware that specific hate groups are spreading misinformation in the hopes of recruiting more members.

A second way of witnessing is to boycott the march and spread the word to the community to do likewise. A notice could be placed in the paper, inviting the public to attend a potluck party at which the history of the group marching could be discussed; a positive action. The more informed people are, the better.

MAKING AND PLAYING DRUMS

Make two little drums. You will need two 28-ounce food cans, spray paint, several thick rubber bands, and a tray for holding the drums so they won't slide when you're playing them. (I use a rubber cat or dog food mat). You will also need glue remover, such as Goo Gone.

1. Remove one end completely on each food can, leaving no sharp metal burrs. Wash and soak off the labels. You may need a glue remover to remove all the glue. Dry off the cans thoroughly.

2. In a well-ventilated area, spray each can with enamel spray paint (choose a color you love) and let dry thoroughly. Enamel spray paints are available at any good hardware or craft store.

3. If you like, once the enamel is completely dry you can stencil designs on the drums using stencils purchased from craft stores. Use a contrasting color of spray enamel to spray the stencil decorations.

4. Once all is dry, wrap several thick rubber bands around the cans near the top of each can (the closed ends) and do the same on each can near the bottoms (the open ends).

5. When you are finished making your two drums, sit at a height where you can comfortably hit your drums with your fingertips. Your forearms should be bent at right angles from your sides.

6. Next time you have a child visiting or are at a social gathering or volunteer commitment, give the child one of the

drums and ask the child to sit facing you.

7. Using your fingertips to hit the drum, tell the child to copy you. Say, "One, two, three, four," hitting the drum with each beat. Then have the child duplicate what you just did.

8. Next say, "*One*-and-*two*-and-*three*-and-*four*," accenting the numerals by hitting them harder. Have the child repeat after you. You can also try what is known as three-quarter time, saying, "*One,* two, three; *one* two three."

In this fashion, make up patterns that grow more complicated as the child learns to hear them, such as, "One, two, *rest*, four; one, two, *rest*, four." As the child becomes more competent, switch roles with you replicating their drum patterns. Finally, put on their favorite music and "accompany" it together on your drums.

AN INTIMATE FAMILY EVENING

Spend the entire evening without using electric lights or devices, like observing Shabbat, the day of rest. Buy a box of votive candles and an equal number of candleholders. Prepare ahead a simple dinner like a stew which only requires heating up.

As soon as everyone is in for the night, turn off all the lights, phones, radios, and computers. Set the candles in candle holders in safe places around the room and on the table. Have dinner with only candles as your source of light.

After eating, move the candles to a comfortable room and ask everyone to take a seat. Go around the room with each person telling a story or singing a song. The stories may be made up on the spot, or they could be from family lore, or they may be old fairy tales or yarns everyone has heard. While each person is talking or singing, everyone else must remain quiet. Keep this up until you go to bed. If possible, use the candles in the bathroom to wash by and in the bedroom to get dressed for bed. Obviously, children should be helped by an adult.

OF DESIRE, LUST, AND RESENTMENT

Do you ever find that you feel jealous of someone you know? If you do, then you know how awful jealousy feels. In your journal, write the person's name on a blank page. Draw a line down the center of the page and in one column, list the things you covet about the person (i.e., they are talented, attractive, financially well-off, beloved by others, etc.).

In the other column, write down your own enviable qualities in comparison to those you envy in that person. On the back of the page, brainstorm a list to try and pinpoint what is causing your envy. What did you discover? Sit with what you have learned for a while.

When your feelings of envy have lessened, make an effort to engage this person in conversation, if possible, keeping in mind what you like about them. Do this several times, if possible. At some point, genuinely compliment them about the trait or skill which they possess of which you are jealous. You may be surprised at the person's response.

COURTESY

When you enter a public space, hold the door open for someone, regardless of what age or gender you or they happen to be. Make eye contact with them and smile. If you have even more time, plant yourself in a busy public space and act as the official door-opener. Busy moms with kids in tow and people with packages or groceries in their arms will be especially appreciative. This lifeline applies to holding elevator doors, as well.

WEATHER ENTHUSIASTS

Explore the weather. If you find yourself stuck in a pattern of weather, use this as a chance to explore all aspects of it. For example, look up the average amount of rain, and snow, for your area over the last decade. Is your present experience typical? If you notice a pattern, find out what could be causing it. Get some other people involved, especially your kids. Make a chart showing the highs and lows for the month, with the dates horizontally arranged on the bottom and the inches of precipitation or the temperatures arranged vertically on the left. You can draw the line in red if it goes above normal or in blue when it goes below.

Go online and find a meteorologist with whom you can speak. You may also try calling the science department at a college. Arrange a trip to speak with them firsthand. Since girls are often overlooked in the sciences, this is particularly valuable for them to experience. Understanding our volatile environment is everyone's responsibility. Only then can we make informed decisions regarding controlling climate change.

WHEN TO YIELD

Look up the word, "acquiesce" in the dictionary. Ask yourself how often do you acquiesce. Do you do it frequently, sometimes, or never: frequently, sometimes…never?

In what circumstances or situations do you acquiesce? Consider whether or not you need to change your behavior.

WITHIN THE SHADOWS

Everyone watches eclipses with a mixture of awe and delight. *Oxford Languages* (formerly *Oxford Language Dictionary*) defines "eclipse" as "an obscuring of the light from one celestial body by the passage of another between it and the observer or between it and its source of illumination." "Eclipse" comes from the ancient Greek word "ekleipein" which translates as "to fail to appear."

Make a list in your journal of the times you have felt "eclipsed" by someone or something else. For example, when you were small, was there a project you worked hard on—a dance recital, a science project, a drawing, or improving your pitching skills for a Little League game? Did a person or an event get in the way of your being noticed or appreciated? Go on to your teenage years and list people or situations that eclipsed you such that you felt obscured. Do the same for each decade of your life. Did someone outshine you at work and get the promotion you wanted? Did your employer go out of business because another country eclipsed the United States by doing superior work more cheaply?

Next, record how you felt in each instance. Were you hurt, angry, or perhaps vengeful towards the body that forced you to "fail to appear?" Finally, make a list of all the times you have eclipsed someone else, intentionally or not. Think about how people can help shine a light on each other's positive accomplishments. In your own personal sphere, how can you assist others to step out of the darkness and be illuminated?

A MOON WITH A VIEW

Go outside while the moon is full and look at it through binoculars. Those of you for whom this is impossible may look at moon photos online, especially when a super moon is in view. "Lean in" with your imagination, so that you are ascending toward the moon. Feel yourself soaring upwards, as if in a flying dream. Keep your focus on the luminous whiteness of the orb as you float through the earth's atmosphere. Feel gravity's bonds slip, along with time's abiding constraint.

Picture yourself landing on the surface of the moon; not like an astronaut, in gray soil, but like a milkweed seed, drifting gently down on a sparkling white surface that feels velvety underfoot. Turn back to our earth. See our planet as an iridescent water bubble full of life. How fragile . . . how irreplaceable. Everything anyone has ever loved is there on Earth. Push off the moon's surface and float home, redoubling your resolve to protect the earth and its creatures.

SAVING ART SAVES CULTURE

Participating in the arts broadens your mind, drawing you out of your own little world into the public. Humans, as primates, are tribal animals who prefer cultures similar to their own. Homo Sapiens have, over the past three hundred thousand years, destroyed the people and culture of smaller, weaker groups. This has led to the more powerful groups' ascendancy.

It is important for us to learn from humanity's past mistakes so that we stop repeating them. In repressing a group's culture, the arts and the languages are attacked since they serve to preserve and unite people.

Pre-20th c. Ireland, still predominantly an oral culture, was prohibited from speaking or teaching Irish by their English conquerors. Celtic harps, a symbol of Ireland, were purposely destroyed.

During Mao Zedong's China's Cultural Revolution, musicians, artists, writers and professors displaying western influences were sent to labor camps to be re-educated.

American enslavers forced their captives to abandon their religions, languages, and foods. The enslaved peoples' rich cultures, histories, musical instruments and songs, stories, and arts were labeled barbaric by their captors.

Native American villages were destroyed, and their languages, dances and manner of dress were prohibited, culminating in the removal of native children from their families to be raised apart from their cultural roots.

The Nazis banned anything Jewish, deriding art, music, and literature created by Jews as decadent. Consider how the arts have helped bring people together. The musical, *Hamilton*, is a prime example, garnering audiences unfamiliar with hip-hop as well as people unfamiliar with Broadway musicals. Where would America be without jazz, country, Broadway, bluegrass, tap, clogging, music festivals, murals, documentaries, great writers, poets, painters, and storytellers?

Become involved in organizations whose goals are to preserve, encourage and assist the arts. A good place to start is to usher at a theater that features live artists. You may find a new interest, hobby and circle of friends. Besides, an usher often gets to hear free concerts in return for their work!

EASTERN FLUTE-PLAYER.

ON FLUENT SPEECH

When we read great speeches, we are often struck by the strength and beauty of their images. We have all heard the myth that Abraham Lincoln wrote the Gettysburg Address on a train ride from the capital city to Pennsylvania. Lincoln never made impromptu speeches. He carefully considered everything he did, understanding that knowledge and education were the keys to a better life. He realized the power of words to move people.

When the space shuttle Challenger exploded in front of the eyes of the world in 1986, the eloquent speech delivered by President Ronald Reagan comforted our grief-stricken nation. Senatorial candidate Barack Obama's 2004 speech at the Democratic National Convention rocketed him into the national spotlight. In 2014, Malala Yousafzai, the youngest recipient of the Nobel Prize, spoke out, advocating for "voiceless children who want change."

Your task is to read these speeches, analyzing why they move us. Here in the United States in the twenty-first century, educated, well-read people with good vocabularies are increasingly viewed as elitists. This has led to the election of officials whose vocabulary and clichés are the equivalent of speech one might expect to hear on a middle school playground. Any meaningful depth or nuances of the speaker's meaning are missing. Read the Gettysburg Address. Pay attention to the poetry of the phrases and the rhythm. Enjoy rolling the lush words around in your mouth like grapes. Vocabulary is the toolkit we use to build understanding.

FREE AND SIMPLE

Get a book or go online to learn how to use your hands to make shadow shapes on the wall. Practice a little every day until you remember how to do all the simple ones and as many of the more complex ones as possible. Once you remember a good number of them, try making up some shapes on your own.

If you practice enough, you will be able to entertain people, both young and old, when you are trapped and waiting around or stuck in elevators, waiting rooms, or in lines. All you need is a light behind you. This is a lot of fun at no cost.

FLOWING THROUGH THE PROBLEM

Everyone must face problems in their lives; they are unavoidable. However, problems can often feel pretty overwhelming. If you are feeling helpless and anxious, you may need to take a mental health break, where you totally remove yourself from worrying about an issue by going to a movie or getting lost in a book. Wrestling with whatever the problem is, chewing it over and over will only exhaust you.

Once you have taken your break, find a quiet place to be alone. Imagine that you are curled up in the womb of The Problem. Practice breathing deeply and relax your muscles. Check your breathing every five minutes as you imagine the problem pressing in all around you. Exhale deeply as you release your muscles even more.

Now picture yourself slipping through The Problem into the daylight. Stand up and stretch your limbs and know that in this new day you are strong enough to find an effective solution.

HELPING OUR FELLOW CREATURES

When we see a creature that is obviously lost or hurt, we have a moral duty to stop what we're doing and help; to act with compassion toward animals. But what is the best way to help and stay safe in the process?

Never approach an animal if it is acting strangely, especially if it is a nocturnal creature roaming about in broad daylight. Likewise, walk slowly away from a snarling dog or an animal with foam in its mouth. Don't touch an injured animal or try to pick it up. Carry an old blanket with you to temporarily cover a hurt animal, if you can do it without getting too close, while waiting for help, as this calms the animal. Call an expert such as your local fish and wildlife game warden or an animal control officer for help and keep track of the animal from a distance.

Prepare yourself to deal with lost or injured pets. Locate your nearest animal hospital or shelter. Call and ask if they take in injured cats, dogs, or wildlife. Often, they can tell you the phone number for places that do. For animals that are not injured, keep a small bag of dry pet treats at home and in your car. A lost pet will often run away from you unless you offer food. Try to get someone from animal control to come pick the animal up while you stay with them. Never chase or approach a frightened dog or cat. If a dog wearing a collar and a license approaches you, wagging and touching you, you can try to fasten a leash on their collar and take them home or to a shelter. Observe posters in your town describing lost animals and keep a lookout for them. There will come a time when your own pet could become lost or injured and might be saved by the kindness of strangers.

LIFE STORIES

Let everyone who will be gathering for a family holiday or reunion know ahead of time that you want their family stories, such as tales of the earliest celebration anyone remembers or favorite memories of relatives who have passed away. Figure out some way to record voices or, better yet, make a video with a soundtrack. Make sure everyone is comfortable with your recording at the event.

Let the little folk tell their stories too. Ask them, what's the best thing they remember about the holiday. What is their favorite food that is always served for the occasion? Especially encourage the oldest members to tell their family tales. These are irreplaceable; they are the very building blocks of families.

EXAMINING COSTLY MISTAKES

Recall a time when you lost the respect or love of a person (or a number of people) because your behavior was heedless, inconsiderate, or unkind. This could have been due to immaturity, illness, jealousy, defensiveness, selfishness, or ignorance.

Fold two pieces of paper (8 ½ x 11 inches) in half widthwise. Place the folds together with one folded paper inside the other, so it looks like a small book, and staple along the fold. The first page of the booklet will be your title page. You can title it when you are done if you like. Open the title page and on the second page, draw a line down the center, creating two columns. In the left column, write the approximate date(s) during which the behavior(s) occurred. On the right, make a list of the various things you did and said that made people turn against you. On the back of that second page, list the people and groups affected by your behavior and one or two words describing how you think your actions made them feel. The third page will be your list of all the reasons you can think of for having acted that way. On the back of this page, list the name(s) of people irrevocably lost to you by your actions: people who have since passed away or who cannot bring themselves to forgive or trust you.

On the last page, write what you are sorry for doing and how you will try to change from this point on. Regard this as a contract with yourself. Sign your name and the date. Close this book.

YOU ARE MOST WELCOME

Politely ask those you see on a daily basis if they have a place to go on holidays when people in your community gather with family to feast and celebrate. Invite someone who might be alone on the holiday to be part of your celebration.

WHOSE VOICE COUNTS?

Find a copy of Thomas Paine's Revolutionary War pamphlet "Common Sense." Published in 1776, Paine's proposal that average white males should govern became, for many colonists, the deciding argument for breaking from England and establishing a republic. The idea that ordinary white males should rule themselves through elected representatives caught fire amongst patriots, leading to the First Continental Congress. Then read John Adams' pamphlet, "Thoughts on Government." Worried that uneducated people would make bad choices, Adams argued for a more conservative government with checks and balances of popular majorities. Next, read the letter Benjamin Banneker (a free person of color) sent Thomas Jefferson (then Secretary of State) stating that the Three-Fifths Compromise and slavery itself violated the ideals of the Declaration of Independence. Banneker's ideas were laid out in his published almanac as well. Finally, the 1848 Seneca Falls Convention, the first woman's rights convention in America, produced a document entitled the "Declaration of Sentiments." This established the goals for the women's suffrage movement. Get a group together to read and discuss these writings.

Draw some parallels to the difficulties Americans have struggled with throughout our history. Ask yourself, "Who should be enfranchised, and why? How is this struggle playing out today?"

PUBLIC THEATER

Go somewhere where there are crowds of people seated at tables, like a coffee shop. Sit close enough to a table that you can clearly hear what the people are saying. Bring your notebook, so you can write things down.

Call one person A, the other B, etc. Put a small plus sign after the females and a zero after the males. For someone you can't identify, write AB. Listen to their conversation. See if you can detect a theme or a story if there is one. Write it down. Which person began it? How does the other person respond? How do they bring the topic to a close? When one person asks a question, does the other listen and respond appropriately? Write it all down like it was a play.

Go to many types of locations throughout the week: a public bus, a park bench, a bar, a playground. Describe the age of the speakers. Once you have gathered at least ten examples of conversations, analyze your results. How many people were really listening to the other person? How could you, a third party, tell?

The next time you have a conversation with someone, apply what you have learned.

I'M SO SORRY

Sincerely apologize to someone for bumping into them, interrupting, or blocking their way. Look them in the eyes. Choose kind, honest words. You may also call or send a note of apology to someone you have wronged in the past. (No texts or emails).

Note: You must accept the fact that you may not be forgiven.

UNSPOKEN MEANING

Use the phrase, "How can I help?" at least three times today. When you use it, notice that your intonation and body language matter. For example, if you emphasize the word "can" and raise your shoulders in a shrug, you imply that you really cannot help, even if you were so inclined.

If you say it in up-speak, with the inflection of your voice rising at the end of the phrase, you might sound like a salesperson; impersonal. Take note of how you sound; look at yourself in a mirror and ask yourself the question.

What makes the question sound as if you really mean it? Imagine someone saying those words to you when you need help.

INANIMATE EXPRESSIONS

The next time you are a passenger in a car at night, bring along a flashlight and a pad and pencil. Take a look at the rear lights of the car in front of you. Imagine the lights as two eyes and the license plate as a nose. The line of the bumper is the mouth.

Make a drawing of what you see; the "face" on the car in front of you, using your flashlight to see your drawing. Use simple shapes: circles, dots, and dashes. You will notice some car's "eyes" look small, like simple dots. Others turn up or down at the ends. Some look angry; some astonished. Some look like they have a pupil!

You don't have to draw the outline of a face; just the "expression" made by the lights, the license, and the bumper. Draw as many as you can. The next time you are in public, take out your drawing and discreetly identify people who look like each of your "faces." Ask yourself, "Which features make this person's face resemble a particular drawing?"

MAKE IT SNOW

Design and cut a snowflake. You need an 8 ½ inch square of paper, a pencil, and a pair of paper scissors.

1. Fold the square in half horizontally, and then fold this vertically, resulting in a 4 ¼ inch square.

2. Hold the folded square with one corner pointing up with the folded sides on the right and the left.

3. Draw a line from the top point to the bottom point.

4. Holding the right-hand corner, fold it towards you until the whole folded edge touches the center line. Repeat with the left side.

5. Cut off the triangular non-folded pieces at the base, leaving a 3 ½ by 4 ¼ inch folded triangle.

6. Fold Each folded edge back along the midline so that you now have a skinny folded triangle.

7. Holding the paper with the right angle to the right, cut ½ inch off of the top at any angle. Draw several small triangles on the left-hand edge, making sure they don't touch the right edge. Draw a triangle on the bottom edge that is ½ inch tall and goes from the left edge to the right. Cut out your shapes and open your snowflake.

Practice cutting out several different shapes. Buy some white paper and whenever you have your hands free, cut a snowflake, the smaller, the better.

Poke a tiny hole in one part and thread a string or thread through it. Tie a knot at both ends. (Fishing line or invisible thread from a sewing store is great for this). With a fine-tipped marker write: "Thank You" in small letters near the center of the snowflake. Carry several snowflakes with you in a plastic sandwich bag. When someone does something nice for you, particularly if they are a stranger, hand them a snowflake.

ELEMENTAL

Let us consider water. Britanica.com/science states that water is the "most abundant substance at the surface of the earth." Much of our bodies consist of it. It is necessary for all living things. Make a list of all the places where water is found naturally on earth. How many of these sites have you seen with your own eyes? How many forms can water take?

Consider that something as gentle and soft as rain can become a rushing river that carves rock, creating structures such as the Grand Canyon. Those of us who are fortunate enough to receive clean water by simply turning a faucet should be mindful of fellow Americans, whose tap water has been polluted with lead or other toxic materials.

Locate sections of our country where industrial malfeasance has resulted in polluted water. What happened in these instances? What would you do if this occurred in your community? Make a list of people in charge of ensuring that your water remains potable. Protect not just your own right to have clean water, but the rights of others.

OFFERING VERSES

Collect poems you like, funny ones or poems with uplifting or thoughtful messages. Print them (noting the author) and put them in a folder. In your travels, when you see someone down on their luck, or an exhausted mom or dad with a bunch of cranky little kids, or anyone who could use something beautiful in their life, offer them a poem and ask, "Would you like a poem? You have your hands full right now, but you can read it later." Give them the poem along with a genuine smile.

US

Go somewhere at lunchtime, even if you only have half an hour, and have something refreshing to drink. Look around you at all the people, talking, rushing, laughing, working on their phones. This is what part of America looks like.

When you are overwhelmed by the cruelty or selfishness in the world, remember all the goodness that is part of most people, including yourself.

INTERGENERATIONAL MIX

Host a music party with *at least* three generations of families; the more families, the better. Kids under the age of ten, people ten to twenty, twenty to forty, forty to sixty, sixty on up. Ask each person to give you a list of music they like ahead of time, including the particular singers, bands, or players who perform the music.

Spend some time hunting down music online. If people have recordings that can be played, all the better. Tell each guest to prepare a few sentences explaining something about their choices; why they chose it, what era it was from, and what was their world like then.

Serve some tasty snacks, sandwiches, and punch, or have people bring something good to share.

TOGETHERNESS

Celebrate with others whenever you can. It's a great way to make friends. During the 1950s, many people joined bowling leagues. The leagues were like clubs for adults to get together. It was common for bowling leagues to hold family picnics and parties where everyone pitched in and made food. The kids spent the day running and playing while the parents drank beer and soda and sat around laughing. It didn't cost much, but everyone had a wonderful time.

In an otherwise lonely world, many towns and cities provide free events where strangers can meet each other. Art openings, block parties, concerts, and parades are places to gather. These days, people are tied to their electronic devices, and it is tempting to "try to get things done," rather than taking time out to be with friends, family, and strangers.

We're always in these little boxes; cars, homes, office cubicles, which separate us from others. As a result, many of us are lonely and depressed. If you can relate to this, find out what is available in your area. Take a risk and go. You have nothing to lose and may gain a whole new world!

ON SPENDING

Consider the word spend. Make a list of all the ways you spend. This can include your free time, leisure time, work hours, your emotional state, your social state or your money. Make several other lists: (a) the ways someone you dislike spends, (b) the same for someone you admire.

Finally, make a list of how you will spend the day, this week, and the rest of the year. Consider all the ramifications of your spending habits. How are you spending your life?

FOR THE RACE

Teach someone a skill this week. You may underestimate how many skills you possess. Do you have a recipe that has come down through your family? Why not share it? Do you play an instrument, build birdhouses, do origami, grow gardens, sell lemonade, *make* lemonade, swim the breaststroke, speak English, Spanish, Mandarin, Cherokee…?

You possess something you may not even realize that is very special. Immortality results from passing on what you have learned. 'Don't know anyone you think would be interested? You are dead wrong! Call up religious groups, clubs, scouts, veterans' groups, homeless shelters, and hospitals. Humans were born to share information. The human race *is*… a relay race! PASS…IT…ON.

EVERYDAY SUPERPEOPLE

If you ride public transportation to get to work take note of the people sitting around you. Think how each day they get up and try to make themselves look and smell nice. Observe how tired people are in the morning and afternoon. Notice that most of the people are quiet. See how vulnerable and gentle everyone seems.

Imagine the hardships your fellow passengers face every day: cranky bosses, deadlines, undependable public transportation, colds...These people are everyday heroes to the children, parents, and spouses who love and depend upon them.

As you exit the train, bus, plane, re-entering the world of noise, competition, and bustle, hold the memory of your fellow commuters close to your heart, where you can pull it out for inspiration when needed in your own heroic day.

OF MUSIC, GLASS, AND WATER

Make a glass instrument. Find a secondhand store or swap shop where you can purchase sets of old wine glasses, the thinner the better. You will need at least 24 glasses (more if possible), a small saucer of water for wetting your finger, and a large pitcher of water. Have a pitch pipe, or a tuning app on your phone, or an in-tune instrument close by.

1. Fill all of the wine glasses halfway. Place eight of them in a line, beginning in the middle of the table.

2. Wet your fingertip and run it around the rim of the first glass until it makes a ringing sound. Experiment until you can achieve a clear note. Next, play a middle C on the pitch pipe, app, or your musical instrument. Tune the first glass to this pitch by either pouring water out of the glass or adding water to it.

3. Make a C major scale by tuning the next seven glasses to D, E, F, G, A, B and C (this C an octave higher than your Middle C).

4. Place seven glasses to the left of your Middle C glass. Working from the Middle C downwards, tune the glasses to: B, A, G, F, E, D, and C (an octave below your Middle C). You should now have, starting from left to right, these notes: C (below Middle C), D, E, F, G, A, B, Middle C, D, E, F, G, A, B, and C (above Middle C).

Now, pick out simple tunes you know to play on the glasses, using the technique explained in step number 2. For "Frère Jacques," play C, D, E, C, C, D, E, C, E, F, G, rest; E, F, G, rest; and so on, wetting your finger as needed.

Find several people to join you. Each will be responsible for playing a particular note or notes. To increase your range, you can play in other keys. For the key of G, you will need F#s instead of Fs. The more complicated the tune, the more glasses you will need.

This is lots of fun to do with kids who can coordinate their fingers enough to make the glasses sound. Did you know that Ben Franklin invented a musical instrument, similar to the one in this exercise, which he called the Glass Armonica? Mozart and other famous composers actually wrote pieces for this instrument! Look it up. Have fun composing and playing.

OVERABUNDANCE

On the next Black Friday, a major U.S. shopping day for holiday bargains, ask your friends and relatives to take the money they would normally spend on your holiday gift and donate it to someone for basic necessities. Many of us don't need more *stuff*.

There are so many people suffering from disasters caused by ongoing poverty, war, and climate change that if each of us could give just this little bit, we could help a lot of people. Charities such as the American Red Cross, Doctors Without Borders, or Habitat for Humanity International are eager to receive donations (and volunteers!) Your nearest food pantry is always grateful for financial help. If you're worried about the merchants losing money, purchase something to donate to local charities, such as shoes, books, or clothing.

A FAUSTIAN BARGAIN

Take note of the fall of current politicians, celebrities, and people in powerful positions. List the mistakes that led to their downfall. Many of them "made a deal with the devil," joining a cause they didn't truly believe in because it seemed to be winning. They rationalized doing something they considered wrong for personal gain, telling themselves, "It's just this once."

What they did may have involved doing something immoral or illegal to advance their boss's goals, thinking the boss would protect them, or they may have been sowing their wild oats, assuming they wouldn't get caught. We are all human and make mistakes. Make a list of five times you have compromised yourself for gain. Celebrities, elected leaders and everyday folks must learn from mistakes and make restitution; if we wish to be part of a healthy society, we should insist upon it. Our children are watching and learning from us.

BORN FREE?

A cat can be a wonderful companion. Stroking a cat has a measurably good effect upon your heart rate, slowing it down. Cats who live on farms can help keep vermin under control in one's barn. But un-spayed, cats can also produce unwanted litters of kittens who become feral.

In the suburbs cats running free create other problems. If he or she poops outdoors, rather than at home in a litter box, he/she is possibly digging up your neighbor's gardens. Cat poop, like dog poop, can incubate disease. Toxoplasmosis Gondii is spread in the feces of felines and can be dangerous to a developing human fetus.

Domestic cats are not wild animals. They decimate the bird populations while having little effect on rats, mice, moles, or chipmunks in the suburbs. People put down poison for rodents. A cat eating a rodent (and the poison) may die a horrible death. Un-neutered cats that run loose are the source of millions of unwanted kittens who are killed in shelters or worse. We love our cats for their beauty, affection, and grace. Give them plenty to do inside. They will reward you with years of love.

A SMALL BOOST

Carry some cash with you when you go shopping. If you see someone at the checkout who is having a hard time finding the right
change, offer them the money. Often, the person is struggling to
find their change purse; sometimes they can't see properly. If they
protest your helping them say, "It's ok. In the past, others have
done this for me."

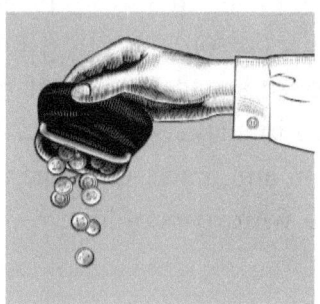

MAKING SCENTS

Hold a smelling bee. Assemble several types of fruit like a banana, a melon, pineapple, strawberry, and lemon. Now gather several assorted flavorings and extracts: vanilla, almond, and orange. Get some chocolate syrup and pour a tablespoonful into a small cup. Next, get spices: cinnamon, cloves, oregano, tarragon, sage, thyme, and rosemary.

Gather a group of people together. Have everyone bring along a sleeping mask or a blindfold. The idea is to have everyone guess what they are smelling without looking. We humans have a weaker olfactory sense than most other animals. We respond more to sweet, salty, and bitter than we do to anything subtle. To enjoy tastes more and appreciate the complexities of food and drink, we need to pay attention to its odor.

See if you can find patterns in the people in your group. Does age or gender factor in on how well you can taste or smell? Once you have done this game, you can move on to more subtle tastes and spices from other cultures.

How many of you have ever smelled orange-flower water, for example? There is a whole unexplored world of scents out there for many of us!

THE SUPPLE MIND

Let us consider the word "change." By the time we hit puberty, we can find it difficult to change our attitudes. Yet, if we don't do it then, it will be even harder to be flexible as we get older. Change may be the one constant in the world. Everything and everyone must change. Rocks get worn down into sand and pebbles, the earth warms and cools, and all life begins and ends.

We become comfortable with things as they are and fear the unknown paths ahead. However, once we learn to embrace change rather than fear it, we can move on more smoothly, both personally and as a society. There is a martial arts style called Baguazhang, which originated in China, in which one uses balance and movement to upset the gesture and harmony of one's opponent. The style is connected to the *I Ching* (*Book of Changes*) and Taoist philosophy regarding the balance between Yin and Yang forces. To the uninitiated, fighters look as though they are twisting away from each other with each movement, avoiding contact. Sometimes, when our culture or people change, it can appear as though they are violently twisting away from what had been experienced for eons. Many of us resist change, but we should consider the fact that what cannot twist and bend breaks.

Today, examine one characteristic of yourself you would like to change. Write it in your notebook. Take one small step...go slowly, but learn to change your behavior or attitude about something. If we remain open and flexible, we will be able to adapt, as well as tolerate the ideas of others.

A WORTHY VIRTUE

Choose one thing in your day with which you will be patient. It could be slow traffic, a cranky baby, an argumentative person, or a task you are having trouble learning. When you feel your anxiety level begin to rise, tell yourself, "Slow down."

WORTH KEEPING

Look up the word, "conserve." Let us consider the implications of this word, which originated in the Latin word, "conservare." "Con" in Latin means with or together. "Servare" means to watch over or keep safe. *Merriam-Webster* defines "conserve" as: to keep in a safe or sound state: to avoid waste or destruction. *Dictionary.com* defines it as: to prevent decay or waste or loss of. Now, compare it with the word "preserve." Preserving something means keeping it untouched or in a pristine state. Conserving means using the resource, but wisely and sparingly.

Make a list this week of remaining pristine areas of America. Google how many pristine areas were part of America 100 years ago, 200 years, 300 years. Now, ask a mathematician, online or in real life, to predict how many unspoiled areas will be left in America in 100 yrs. Next, make a list of resources animals need in order to live. Involve some friends in this project. Get those mathematicians involved in this part, if you like, too. Make a prediction about how long humans have before we run out of water, clean air, and food at our present growth rate.

Keeping in mind that conserving really means acting together to prevent destruction, identify policies that are endangering the preservation and conservation of our planet and all who depend upon its resources for life. Volunteer to assist associations working to save our land, water, air and climate.

YOUR ANIMAL

Figure out which animal you are most like. There may be more than one. Some people look like certain animals; others share characteristics with a specific species. Some similarities are so blatantly obvious that the minute you point them out, people say, "Oh… yeah!" Your animal does not have to be beautiful or virtuous. Each creature is an important part of our ecosystem and is therefore worthy of respect. I have seen warthogs, horses, foxes, and even three-toed-sloths in the shape of humans. One's animal may not always be a mammal; it could be an insect, fish, crustacean, or reptile. Once you have found your animal(s), find out all you can about them; are they domestic, endangered, extinct, or timid? Collect pictures of your animal. Ask someone who knows you well if they can see the relationship. Practice figuring out others' animals when you are in public. For example, do you have a friend who is big like a polar bear, or swift as a red-tailed hawk? Do you know someone who is as fierce and sly as a fisher cat? Finally, find someone you trust and tell them your animal as you see it. If they accept your idea, try helping your friend guess their own animal. If you become good at this, you will find that people are startled at first when you point out someone's animal, and after consideration, often agree. Then get people to identify with and protect their own animal(s). Some folk will become very involved, learning all they can about their animal, and even joining causes to protect and support their creature.

VERACITY

Make it your business to read different news sources this week. Regardless of your political viewpoint, make a list of five sources you use to obtain news. If you find that you rely only on talk radio or social media, begin asking people you respect for other sources. Compile a list of recommendations and check each out. Next, when a big news event occurs, compare the coverage in several of the sources you have found; sources considered liberal as well as conservative. See how each covers the same story.

Finally, develop the habit of fact-checking your news, instead of accepting as truth what you hear from people or sources with whom you usually agree. Much angst is caused by false news coverage geared towards sensationalism. Get the facts.

PRINTING PRESS WORKED AT BY FRANKLIN
IN LONDON.

THOSE WHO MATTER

Take a piece of paper and make four columns; five if you are 60 or older. At the top of the page over the first column, write Childhood. Over the second, Adolescence; the third, Young Adulthood, the fourth, Middle Years, and last, Advanced Years.

Spend some time on each column, looking at photos from those periods of your friends, relatives, and associates with whom you have lost touch. List a person in each category who, at the time, was an important influence.

Now, using the internet, try finding the person. You may have to contact others you knew at the time to help you locate the person you are seeking. The older you are, the more likely it is that the person may have passed away.

Take notes as you search. Enjoy re-establishing ties with people who were part of your life long ago. People will not be the same as you remember them, nor will they necessarily share your beliefs, but some will not have altered significantly.

TRUE VALUES

Make a value chart. The word "value," from the Latin, valere, meaning to be of worth or strength, can refer to the lightness or darkness of a color. You will need a piece of white illustration board 12 inches long by 3 inches high, a pencil, a ruler, 2 jars of opaque poster paint: one black, one white, a box of wooden craft mixing sticks, and 2 small watercolor brushes. An inexpensive white mixing palette is nice, but a white china plate or plastic surface will do. Additionally, buy a roll of low-tack painter's tape an inch wide.

1. Tape your board at all four corners to a working surface, and draw two horizontal lines, one an inch below the top and one an inch above the bottom. Tape above the top line and below the bottom, leaving a white strip 12 inches long.

2. Next, draw a vertical line 1 inch from each side and tape both vertically 1 inch from the edge, reducing the white strip to 10 inches long.

3. With pencil and ruler, divide the white strip into 10 boxes, each 1-inch square.

4. Working from left to right, Paint the first box pure white. This is value number 1. Paint the last box black. This is value number 10.

5. Paint each value from left to right a bit darker until it reaches black.

HINTS: Wash brushes completely clean with soap and water in-between mixing and dry them. Mix each value in your mixing Palette or your white china or plastic mixing surface, mixing enough paint to cover one square. Let each square dry thoroughly before painting the next. Once your chart is thoroughly dry, gently remove the tape. Write the value number under each square.

Your goal is to create a perfectly smooth transition from white to black, where value number 5 is exactly mid-way between black and white. Once your chart is complete, you can begin guessing the value of objects, checking to see how close you came by holding your value chart next to the object you have chosen.

Begin with something easy, such as the value of a painted wall. Squinting makes identifying values easier by the amount of light entering your retina. Where do most human skin values fall? If you have ever tried to paint a portrait, you will know how hard it is to determine a person's correct skin value, regardless of their color. Values change depending upon where the light shines.

PAUSE AND REFLECT

Pretend your teeth are the gates to your castle. Plan well before you open them. Take time during the day to listen to what people say to you. Before responding, inhale, smile, scratch your nose, or murmur, "Ummm." This gives you time to consider your next statement. The pause is especially useful at parties, where people blurt out things or become involved in arguments they will regret. You are the queen/king of your own castle. The wise ruler thinks ahead and chooses battles carefully.

A GOOD LOOK

How do you see yourself? Take a large hand mirror, or better yet, an un-framed square mirror panel, and hold it at right angles to another mirror, such as a bathroom or full-length mirror. Look at your reflection where the two mirrors touch, moving the mirror until you can see your face reflected fully. This is not the reflection you see in the mirror every day; it is the way others see you.

In your journal, make a list of ten adjectives describing each part of your reflection. Now, next to each, write down your impression of each part that you have listed, describing its location. For example, is your right eye higher than your left? If so, did you know that? Does your smile go upwards on one side of your mouth? Lastly, do a little drawing, showing the shape of your hair, your face, your eyes, nose, and mouth. In your travels, take note of others' faces, observing similarities and dissimilarities.

THE THOUGHTFUL ONES

Consider the word "gracious." Look it up in the dictionary. When was the last time you were gracious towards someone? Think of the people in your life. Which of them would you describe as gracious? Can you think of five kind acts you observed in the last week…the last month? In people we do not personally know, we can only guess that they are gracious by observing their actions. Think of public personalities, like movie stars, politicians, and radio hosts. Which of them seem considerate and why?

Graciousness is one of the glues that holds cultures together by modeling civil behavior. Be mindful, in your travels, of ways in which you can be gracious towards others. For example, if you see someone struggling to get a stroller through a door or up a flight of stairs, offer your help. Pony up the change for someone who is stuck in a checkout line and can't find their wallet or is short a few quarters.

The enemy of graciousness is fear of getting involved. Get involved. Don't be fearful.

MULTI-LINGUAL OPPORTUNITIES

If you live in a community where the majority speak more than one language, and you speak only English, use this as a chance for you and your kids to broaden your skills and your minds by learning the language of your neighbors. If the language is a commonly studied European language such as Spanish, French or German, you may study it in a class at a community college. If the language is not offered in your local school or college, there are now online courses in just about every language.

Call your local community center, YMCA, churches, mosques, synagogues, and schools to see if they would be interested in hosting a class that teaches the language you wish to learn. Many Americans only speak English. Europeans learn several as a matter of course since they interact with the countries that border theirs. We have an opportunity to listen to our neighbors, attend community functions where English is not predominant, shop and eat in restaurants with people who speak the language we'd like to know. Learning to communicate in another language not only empowers us by challenging our brains, it enables us to better understand others and appreciate their cultures.

BRAND NEW FRIEND

Make a new friend from someone you like or with whom you exchange small talk within your daily routine. Look up some of the newest movies that are coming out. The next time you exchange pleasantries with this person, ask if they've seen one of the movies. Find one neither of you have seen and say, "Hey…we should go see this movie! Would you like to see it with me? We could meet at the theater…It would be fun!"

TOKENS OF LOVED ONES

Go to an art store or go online and find some quick-setting casting material. You are going to make a handprint as you did in elementary school. You will need foam board at least 4 feet long and 3 feet wide, a ruler or tape measure, a piece of 8 ½ by 11 inch paper and a pencil, a sink in which to wash your hands, a roll of duct tape, a piece of aluminum foil 2 feet by 2 feet, cooking spray, a plastic paint bucket and a paint stirrer for mixing the plaster and a roll of absorbent paper towels.

1. Measure from the longest finger to the heel of your hand along the palm and add 2 inches to this measurement. Next, lay your hand comfortably on a table so it is relaxed.

2. Measure the distance from the top of your thumb across the back of your hand to the top of your pinky finger and add 2 inches. These measurements will be the length and width of the box you will build in which you are going to pour your plaster.

3. Cut a piece of foam board for the bottom of the box using your measurements. Cut four side pieces at least 1½ inches tall that are the length and width of your box and tape them to the outside edges of the base using duct tape on both inside and outside seams and corners to make your box watertight, like a little swimming pool. Line it with foil and spray lightly with cooking oil spray so the mold will be more easily released.

4. Follow the directions on your casting material to make an impression of your hand. Once the material has set, re-

move the plaster cast by gently lifting the foil.

5. When the plaster is cool and completely dry, gently clean the oil off with a paper towel. Take it to a framer and have them make a box frame with glass. This will become a treasured heirloom for your family long after you have passed on.

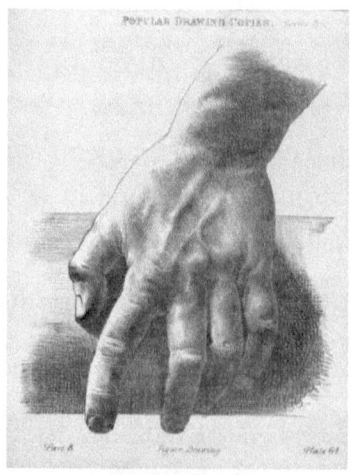

THE LONG AND SHORT OF IT

In a notebook, write at the top of one-page, Short-term Problems. On this page, you will list the everyday annoying tasks that you can complete that day, such as calling for doctor appointments, returning items in the mail or at stores; whatever you deem to be nagging you that isn't part of your daily routine.

On the next page, write, Long-term Problems. These will be things you should but don't want to do, like making difficult personal decisions, having that uncomfortable discussion with someone, changing a habit or routine, etc. Do not include political problems in this.

In order to be healthy and of use to the world, we must first organize our own houses as best we can. Each time you accomplish something on either list, check it off. Use the lists to look back at your successes and celebrate your achievements.

INCREDIBLE LIGHTNESS

Take a few minutes to walk alone somewhere outside. Look around you, paying attention to your environment. Breathe deeply, noting the way the air smells. Note your posture; are you caving in upon yourself?

Pretend you are a marionette, suspended by a string running upwards from the top of your head. Let the rest of your body hang below, meaning your head and shoulders should not bend forward and your back should curve gently at the waist.

Enjoy the feel of your body aligning itself under your head. Return to your regular world, remembering to feel that string suspending your body's weight.

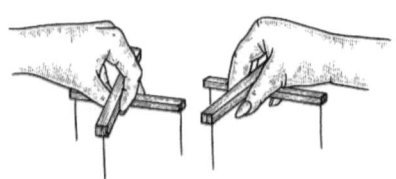

MAINTAIN, SUSTAIN

Many of us are in a state of constant over-stimulation. We are at a point at which our bodies are always involved with our phones or our computers. Both news and social media overwhelm us with information, much of which is designed to arouse us. The human body isn't designed to be in full-drive mode without long rest periods. Consequently, we are shorting out, like over-loaded sockets.

Note in your journal how much time you spend on all your devices. Then, take a mental health break by scheduling time away from the news. Set some personal boundaries regarding the use of social media. Go see a movie. Read. Take a walk. Renew yourself. Renew live contact with others.

Those in the helping professions, whether doctors, nurses, social workers, teachers, therapists, police, firemen and women, are especially vulnerable since their jobs are often high stress to begin with. Increasingly, people find themselves burning out over time, reducing their own effectiveness.

Once you have totaled the hours you devote per day to your own devices, ask your friends and family members to do this exercise; then compare notes. Discuss the effect this over-use is having on your lives and your health. Enact a change.

IN YOUR OWN WORDS

Get a box of stationery paper 8 ½ inches by 11 inches. Fold the paper in half twice, creating four 4 ¼ by 5 ½ inch pages. Cut along the fold, creating four pages. Fasten the pages together by stitching the spine with quilting thread. This will give you eight writing surfaces.

Repeat until you have enough pages for a month of daily entries. Write an entry each day, making a new folio each month. Be sure to date your entries. This is your diary. Each evening, describe your day, noting anything you learned and everything you succeeded in accomplishing; however small.

ADDRESSING OFFENSIVE OBJECTS

In your travels, you may find some racist or sexist "tchotchkes," (Yiddish for unnecessary decorative objects) for sale. These are insulting, hurtful cartoons and images, caricaturing people because of their color, sex, or ethnicity. When you return home, find out all you can about the object you saw. Educate yourself.

Become familiar with the ways in which various groups of people were caricatured in the past and the present. Now, as you go about your days, if you find that you or others are being objectified or ridiculed, don't let it stand. Speak up for yourself and others.

CANINE CLEAN-UP

Dog owners and friends of dog owners should carry a roll of poop bags. They're cheap. You can buy them just about anywhere that sells pet supplies. There are little pouches available for the rolls that can hang from your belt. When your dog poops, put your hand into the empty bag, mitten-style, grab the poop, and pull the bag inside-out. Your hand remains clean, you knot the bag, bring it home, and dispose of it. Some parks provide disposal receptacles.

"Disgusting," you say? "Why not just let it decompose where it lands? It's fertilizer, right?" First of all, what *is* disgusting is stepping in dog poop some irresponsible person didn't pick up. Second, flies lay eggs in dog poop and someone walking barefoot can pick up roundworms, hookworms, whipworms, or Giardia. Other dogs can contract Parvo from dog feces. Dog poop doesn't decompose quickly, and it does not fertilize anything. So, scoop that poop. Oh,... and just bagging it then leaving the bag for someone else to step on not only gives all dog owners a bad name but contributes to the plastic litter which winds up in trees and in water. If you are the friend of an irresponsible dog owner or see one who won't pick up after their pet,... SPEAK!!!

SOOTHING SOLES

Give someone with sore feet the gift of a foot rub. You will need a basin of warm water for soaking the feet (a dishpan is good) a hand towel for drying, and some neutral skin lotion. Seat the person comfortably in a chair low enough so their feet touch the floor. Don't make them bend forward in the seat; prop a pillow behind their back if needed. Soak their feet for five minutes, then dry with the towel.

Begin with the toes, rubbing them upwards towards the ankle. Bend them, together, upwards and downwards, slowly and VERY carefully. Then pull on each toe. Move to the ball of the foot, massaging with both thumbs. Then do the same with the arch. With very gentle strokes, while holding the sole of the foot in both hands, rub the top of the foot upwards with both thumbs. Continue up the front of the ankle and around to the sides of the foot. Cupping the foot with both hands again, rub into the bottom of the heel with your thumbs. Now, with one hand, Stroke upwards on both sides of the Achilles tendon. With both hands, stroke the ankle upwards from the sides of the heels. Finally, massage in a small bit of your skin cream.

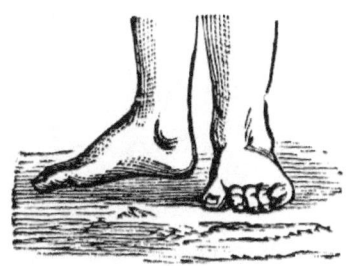

OUR LIMITED VIEW

Stand before a mirror. Touch the bridge of your nose with both index fingers. Keeping your eyes locked on those of your reflection, slowly move your index fingers along the tops of your eyelids towards the sides of your eyes. Notice how much you can see of your index fingers as they move, keeping your eyes straight ahead. Where do you lose sight of them?

Now place your index fingers at the side-most parts of your eyes. Slowly move your hands away from your head. Can you see your fingers? Do you need to move them forward in order to see them? We primates have a limited view of things unless we turn our heads. We also have a blind spot where our optic nerves enter the retina of each eye. We make lots of judgments based only on what we *do* see, which can lead to errors.

Remember this when you think you are sure of what you have seen. Turn your head, the next time you are in a room, on a street, at the ocean. Pay attention to details when you walk through a crowd. Could you describe some of the people you passed? Could you describe the way your loved one's hair looked this morning? Can you remember what your parents' eyes looked like?

THE LIVES INSIDE

If you are driving on snow or ice, especially if visibility is bad or it is night, stay an extra car's length away from the person ahead of you. Remember the rule: for every ten miles of speed, you add another car's length to your following distance.

When you come to an intersection, assume that others won't be able to stop. Plan for what you will do if you or someone else skids. If you yield the right of way, flash your lights twice to signal the other person.

Remember that there are lives all around you inside of those cars; lives that matter just as much as yours. Drive with the intent of protecting yourself as well as others.

KEEPERS

In many religions, we are instructed to be our brother's/sister's keepers. Spend some time thinking about this. Ask yourself if you agree with that statement. Were there instances in your own life where you acted upon this?

Write down on a small slip of paper a list of times someone has kept you out of danger or trouble. Write their names, if you know them; these people who saved you from getting hurt, committing a folly, or set you straight. Reflect upon others throughout history who have been their brothers'/sisters' keepers, who have sacrificed or risked themselves to provide hiding places for innocent people running for their lives.

Read the history of the Underground Railroad, the people who sheltered the Jews of Europe escaping the Holocaust, and more recently, Paul Rusesabagina of Rwanda who led 1,268 people to safety, at his own peril. Consider how far you would go to aid someone in peril.

There are many small ways we can all come to the aid of strangers every day. When we help others, we reinforce the idea that we have the power to effect change in the world as well as ourselves.

NEW YEARS WISHES

In your notebook on two separate pages list: Wishes for the New Year. On one page, write the heading, Personal and Local. These are wishes you make for yourself, your family, friends, and community. On the second page, write, Country and World.

Find at least five people to do the same exercise, then compare your wishes. Now, get together and brainstorm over how to achieve them. Choose one from each page to concentrate on.

SERVING EACH OTHER

If you provide a service or sell things for a living, make sure that both parties are aware of the terms of the sale. Provide those terms in writing for your customers. If anyone contacts you with questions or says they don't understand something on your website, it is far better to call the customer back than to email them. Trying to answer questions in an endless volley of emails can result in confusion and misunderstandings.

If you are, yourself, a customer ordering something online, make sure you get a street address and a customer service telephone number before you spend money. Life is short and precious and should not be wasted arguing, either over poor service or unreasonable demands.

ENDOWING THE ARTS

The next time someone says that we should eliminate the National Endowment for the Arts, read them a quote or two from those who have gone before us regarding art's importance. Here are a few to start with:

"The man that hath no music in himself, nor is not moved with concord of sweet sounds, is fit for treasons, stratagems, and spoils. The motions of his spirit are dull as night, and his affections dark as Erebus. Let no such man be trusted." Wm. Shakespeare (The Merchant of Venice).

"I do not want the arts for a few, any more than education for a few or freedom for a few." Wm. Morris.

"I must study politics and war that my sons may have the liberty to study Mathematics and philosophy, geometry, natural history, naval architecture, navigation commerce, and agriculture, in order to give their children a right to study painting, poetry, music, architecture, statuary, tapestry, and porcelain." John Adams.

"A mushroom rises from wreckage, death, and rot, aerating the earth. So, art feeds on oppression, hate, and bigotry, sending its own spores of life to colonize the darkest places with hope." Bobbie Wayne.

A DIFFERENT CONTEXT

Sit on the floor. Look around. How has your perspective changed from when you stand or sit on a chair? Spend some time in various rooms at this height. What is it like trying to do things? How do others appear? How does it feel looking up at people who are speaking down to you?

Use your newfound knowledge when you speak to people not at eye level with you. Understanding that your perspectives are not the same helps us see how people's perception of reality can be different from each other's.

WHAT'S THE PROBLEM?

Think of someone who has power over you, such as a boss or a teacher. Does this person always seem to be finding fault? Ask yourself and others you trust if they think that you are doing anything to annoy the boss/teacher. If the answer is no, request a meeting with the person. Explain that you feel they are displeased with your performance. Be prepared to state examples to support your claim. If they give you legitimate ways to improve, listen carefully and take notes. Thank them for speaking with you. Then work hard to show them you have taken their suggestions seriously.

However, should they totally deny any ill feelings towards you, thank them anyway. At least you have politely pointed out your perception. This may correct the problem or not. If *they* are the problem and simply treat people badly, ask yourself, "What is this person getting out of behaving this way?" Understanding someone who has power over you can help you find a way to deal more effectively with them.

Some people have themselves been treated badly and perpetuate this by treating others unkindly. Showing *genuine* concern for them, (not kissing up) smiling, treating them as if they were nice can sometimes help. One must stand up to genuinely mean people, however. Protect yourself by keeping a daily journal in which you record the particulars of bullying, discrimination or sexism. Do not live a life of suffering. Speak up for yourself and for others.

SINCERELY, ME

Make a list of people you know who could use a friend. These can be people who live alone, relatives or not, or people you see on a regular basis in your travels. If there are neighbors who are empty nesters add them to your list.

Go out and find the best cards you can, ones with meaningful, kind messages. Write a personal note on each one, saying something nice about the person and asking if they would be interested in your paying them a visit.

Either mail or hand-deliver the cards. If they respond, you might invite them to come over for coffee or tea.

SLEEP PRIMING

Every evening, before you go to bed, spend an hour or more reading or doing something that makes you happy. Do not watch the news or read troubling stories. Find something to do that takes your mind away from stress and worries.

Turn your phone off and establish deadlines for accepting calls at night. Stimulating drinks that contain caffeine can lead to sleeplessness in some individuals. Alcohol, while a depressant, disrupts normal sleep patterns. Maintaining the same bedtime trains your body to be ready to sleep.

Make a sleep journal, listing: target bedtime, actual bedtime, quality of sleep, awakening time, and an area for describing the preceding evening, food, drinks and activities. Keep this journal for several weeks. It will give you a clear picture of your sleep habits.

When you are actually in bed, don't review the day or predict or plan the next; rather, pay attention to the sound of your breathing. The rhythm of your own breathing will soothe you and help you relax your muscles. A good night's sleep is important for clear thinking and actions. Keeping oneself strong and healthy is essential if one wants to work for the good.

PORTRAIT OF MYSELF AS A SHOE

Take the shoes you wear most often and place them on a table where you can get a good look at them. On a pad, write down the following questions: Are they worn down, and if so, where? (i.e., the heels, toes…)

If your shoes were a portrait of a person, what would that person look like? Where have these shoes taken you? Where would you like these shoes to take you in the future? What is stopping you?

THE LANGUAGE OF MUSIC

Treat yourself and a friend to a concert. This should be someone with an attention span of an hour at least. Much of America's musical influences came from other countries and has been adapted and absorbed.

If you or your guest know your family's heritage, it can be fun to find musical ensembles that perform music your ancestors might have played or heard before they came to America. This is particularly true of people whose families have been here for generations. For example, some Americans have never heard Italian opera or traditional Irish music, having grown up hearing only Italian-American pop singers or Irish-American music written by professional songwriters in Tin Pan Alley. The many diverse countries of Africa have their own instruments and music, largely unknown to Americans of African descent. The same is true of Asia's rich and diverse musical traditions which go un-explored by Asian Americans.

Music is the most basic of languages. People who don't speak each other's language can still communicate through music. Go to live concerts! The whole world of music is out there, waiting to be discovered by everyone.

SAYING NO

Learn to say no to unreasonable requests. These can come from family members, friends, community, clubs, schools, or religious organizations. Only when you feel comfortable denying requests can you know that you are sincere when you say yes. Examine your priorities.

Keep a journal for a week, noting the time spent on various activities. Then, on a separate page, pick out the things you did nearly every day, such as eating meals, walking the dog, preparing lunches for school or work, and helping kids with homework. Add all the time these activities take and find the average time, recording it under Daily Tasks. Next, do likewise with time you spend shopping for food and necessities. Record this average under Weekly Necessities. If you regularly transport yourself or your family to and from work, clubs, sports, health, or religious services, calculate the average time spent, recording it under Commuting. Now, add these three column's totals together and record this number under Essentials. Finally, add up the leftover weekly hours spent on social media, practicing and learning new skills, visiting friends, volunteering, or whatever you spent time doing, and record the average number of hours per week under Elective.

Once you have your average number of hours spent per week on Daily Tasks, Weekly Necessities, Commuting, and Elective, you will have a clear picture of how your time is being used. Then, choose to make choices which make your life more satisfying.

THE COST OF FREE SPEECH

When people are prohibited from speaking out about disturbing events in their lives, they can develop depression, anger or anxiety. Spend some time thinking about freedom of speech and a free press. Investigate the history of free speech in America. Take notes of the times this right was threatened, by whom and why. Look up the results.

Are there forces and circumstances at play today which could lead to the repeal of these constitutional rights? Discover what is at stake in America when freedom of speech and the press is threatened. Talk with others about how they view freedom of speech.

GIVE A LITTLE WHISTLE

Practice whistling. If you can't whistle, find someone who can and ask them to teach you. This is a good thing to do at family gatherings, like Thanksgiving, instead of arguing over politics. If you *can* whistle, find someone who can't and offer to teach them.

If you are stuck waiting somewhere with restive children around, start whistling a tune people know, such as, "Twinkle Twinkle Little Star." Some people will smile if you do it with bravado! Then ask the crowd in general, "Ok, who can whistle?" This will definitely get a reaction. Start whistling "Yankee Doodle," or "Happy Birthday," nodding towards people to encourage them to join you.

Your goal is to get people to join you and whistle together. If you find yourself in a crowd of hams, divide the song up and have people harmonize or take solos.

BELIEF

The threat of global destruction is currently raising the level of anxiety around the world. Much of the conflict centers on our conflicting religious beliefs. We can become passive and depressed, cast blame on people who do not share our particular faiths, or we can develop understanding.

Throughout history, for good or bad, humans have organized their behavior around particular theologies, developing morals, mores, laws, customs, and punishments according to these beliefs. Problems occur when these various belief systems are used to validate the subjugation or annihilation of others who don't share our faith.

Choose three beliefs to examine. These can be archaic or contemporary, but if you are a person of faith, choose creeds with which you are unfamiliar. Take note of where and when they originated. How long did each particular doctrine last? Who or what was venerated? What were the major benefits believers attained? What were the drawbacks? Was the belief system used to oppress others? If so, who; what was the outcome? What did the three beliefs have in common?

Read the news, paying attention to conflicts or intolerance connected to religious beliefs. Lastly, take a look at American history and its relationship with religion. What positive and negative effects has religion had on our own country?

Examining our own beliefs and faiths as well as those of others leads to a better understanding of behavior. American law mandates both freedom of religion and separation of church and state. If we wish to enact and enforce laws, we must be willing to compromise with one another, which requires understanding the deeply held beliefs that motivate us. We may not feel as if we can control world events, but respecting each other's core beliefs, practicing tolerance, and working together for a just country allows us to assume an active role in our own future. This places us in a position of power.

IT DOESN'T COST MUCH

Carry with you a small first-aid kit, available at any drug or camping store. This way, you can offer assistance to anyone with a small injury. Children often fall and cut themselves. Nothing dissolves borders between people like offering a brightly colored band-aid to someone with a crying child. Be sure to always have hand sanitizer, as well.

A man filling his tank got sprayed with gasoline when the pump failed to shut off. The person behind him got out of their car and asked if he would like some hand cleaner and paper towels, which the sprayed man gratefully accepted, looking both surprised and pleased. His young son hung out the back window wearing a big smile. A bottle of hand sanitizer is worth ninety-nine cents. Helping and trusting one another is worth everything.

YOUR INNER SEGOVIA

Learn to play an instrument. If you have difficulty hearing pitches and yet wish to play music with others, try an autoharp. These zither-like instruments can be tuned with an electronic tuner which will tell you if a string is in tune or not. Many cultures play some form of zither. The autoharp has a set of labeled dampeners with felt pads. These pads allow only the appropriate strings that form the chord to ring when one strums. When you press down on the C chord bar, for example, and strum the strings, you will only hear those notes that make up a C chord. Autoharps stay in tune better than many stringed instruments. If you have a book of tunes, all you have to do is play the chords as listed and strum as you, or another person, sings or plays the melody. Find a musician who will play along with you to help you get started. You can purchase used autoharps online for a reasonable price. There are online tutorials to help you become competent or a virtuoso. They are wonderful instruments to use for accompaniment in singing with children or at assisted living facilities.

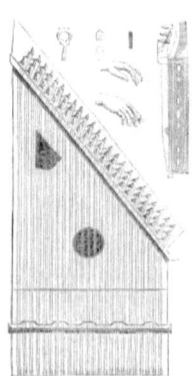

NOT WHAT WE APPEAR TO BE

Stand naked before a full-length mirror. Ask yourself, "Is the person I see in the mirror consistent with my self-image?" Take note of your posture. Do you slouch or stand straight?

Put on a robe and pay special attention to your face. What is your normal expression? Do your eyes appear interested, engaged, or defeated? It is said that humans are the only animals with self-awareness. While I don't buy that, I do believe humans have been given a high degree of self-awareness so that we may improve and correct things about ourselves over our long lives which will benefit all our fellow creatures.

Now look at the person in the mirror. Does that person appear to be defensive or angry? Is your natural expression a frown? Set a goal for yourself: relaxing your forehead. Check yourself every once in a while, with a concealed pocket mirror to see if you are settling back into a frown.

If you rarely smile, you may practice smiling at home before your mirror. At first, it will feel strange, but if you do it enough, you will be able to switch from a tense or angry-looking person to someone who is open and welcoming. You may even find that you breathe more easily. Your facial muscles will automatically soften since it takes more muscular effort to frown than it does to smile. Others will begin to find you more approachable.

BETTER THAN YOURS

The day after the murder of Dr. Martin Luther King Jr, third-grade teacher from Iowa, Jane Elliot, divided her all-white class into two groups: those with brown eyes and those who had blue. For a day, the brown-eyed group were treated with more respect, extra privileges, treats, and play time. The blue-eyed group wore special collars for easy identification.

Both groups adapted to their new status, believing negative propaganda about the "inferior" group. The next day, teacher Elliot switched the groups, treating the blue-eyed children as "superior" and the brown-eyed group as second-class citizens. Once again, they readily accepted the new stereotypes.

Her class of third graders reunited in 1984 and related how they were teaching their own children about tolerance and discrimination. Miss Elliot's exercise, they said, had changed their lives. In 1985, PBS's series, "Frontline" made a documentary about the experiment which is still available to watch. Anyone can replicate this exercise with adults who, unfortunately, are easily convinced of their own or another person's superiority or inferiority, depending upon the circumstances.

Once we become aware of this flawed perception and how easily it can destroy our lives and our communities, we can arm ourselves against it. Watch the video and read about the study. Discuss it with your kids. In helping to heal the cancer of intolerance, we heal ourselves, as well.

HAVE I A DREAM?

Suggest to your friends that they write a list of their dreams for the future. Once everyone has made their list, ask if they would be willing to share. People may laugh and tell you something facile like, "I just want a vacation in Hawaii."

You can have fun going around the group telling about your wishes and hopes. If it feels right, suggest that people really think about what their big dreams are, not just for themselves and their families, but for their communities and for the world. Ask everyone to write something down overnight and bring it on a future date to read to the group.

A HAND UP

Volunteer to help the often-overworked teachers at our public schools. You may not have any experience with teaching or with kids, but all you need is patience, a sense of humor, and a willingness to learn. You might end up using one of your own skills, such as music, art, drama, sports, or an interest in languages, math, science or history.

If you like kids and are willing to listen and be respectful, you can make a difference. Schools for children with special needs are good places to volunteer. Kids with intellectual challenges require lots of individual attention. Plan which age group you would prefer to work with. Call the public schools in your area to learn about volunteer opportunities. Schools for kids with special needs or intellectual challenges can be found online.

Many kids just need some extra tutoring in a subject to get ahead or to keep up. Make a list of all your strengths and mention them when you volunteer. Be sure to ask what will be required of you when you are interviewed.

SPEAK OUT

The next time one of life's many small irritations occurs, speak up about it. For example, if you are in a public place, such as a movie theater, and there is a problem with the focus or the sound, be the person who quietly finds someone to correct the problem.

If the issue concerns a purchase, such as eggs that are broken, food that you brought home, only to find it spoiled, or a defective item, such as a stained or torn garment, call the store and ask for the person in charge. Ask them their name. Explain politely how you have been wronged and how the store can make it up to you (replacing the article, a refund, etc.). Once the situation has been corrected, call the person back and thank them for helping you.

SOLACE IN ORDER

We live in chaotic times. Look around your house/office/studio/barn/factory, wherever you spend lots of time. Pick out one thing which is really dirty, messy, or unorganized. Decide upon a time in which you will clean and organize it.

Messiness and not being able to find things easily contribute to depression. Pare down the items in the area, if you can, deciding if you really need them. Don't pick too large a project or you will give up or avoid doing it. Play some music while you work. Enjoy the feeling of wiping away old dirt; of making things better in this one little part of your life.

PIECE YOUR OWN WORLD

Make a collage. You will need a stiff piece of ¼ inch plywood, a standard frame size, on which to glue your collage and a large assortment of illustrations, photographs, or magazine pictures. Good paper scissors are a must. A glue gun is helpful but other glues may be used. You may choose to use a background in the form of wallpaper, sheet music, or anything with an interesting pattern. Additionally, assemble some light-weight three-dimensional objects to add. These could be small plastic figures, pieces of metal or glass, strings, yarn, or pieces of jewelry.

1. Spend a week or more collecting your treasures. Make sure they speak to you. Start playing with the objects on your stiff background, moving them around until you like their positions. The flat photos and background can be laid down first. Photos can be turned in any direction. You may wish to cut the photos or leave them as is.

2. Next, add your three-dimensional object(s). Have fun placing things in the little world you are creating.

3. Does your collage have a theme or seem to tell a story or is it an abstract composition? Once you are satisfied with your placement, glue things down. You may have to wait for your glue to set up before finishing.

4. Lastly, add any other objects you feel will bring the collage together. Ask yourself how your eye travels around the collage: Does it move rapidly or slowly? Does your world make the viewer want to linger and explore? Once everything is set up, show the collage to others, writing down what they see and feel when they look at your creation.

TAKE NOTE

When you are standing near someone with either a dog or a baby, smile at the person and ask them how old their dog/baby is. The person may begin a conversation with you. Seek people of different ages, races, or gender from you because pets and babies are something many people have in common. They provide excellent conversation starters.

CHARMING YOUR BOGGART

Pick out something you can't change that has you worried, angry, or is making you anxious. This may be related to the world, the country, or your own individual life. In one or two sentences, explain the essence of the upsetting issue.

Your task is to imagine the problem ending in the funniest, most ludicrous, absurd, or ironic scenario. If you are a droll individual, you may do this naturally. If not, you may need a bit of practice. The Beatles were masters at this, as were many vaudevillians, such as Charlie Chaplin.

Professor Lupin in J. K. Rowling's incredible *Harry Potter* series used the incantation, "Riddikulus" as a charm against a Boggart (your worst fear assuming a shape). The charm causes the boggart to change its shape into one that is funny to the caster; thus, neutralizing its fearsomeness.

Do not take this exercise lightly. Humor is one of the greatest weapons against bullies, the unjust and tyrants; it is the balm we use to soothe the rawness of days. Humor is the great leveler, the sword of the meek.

YOUR PERSONAL HEALTH RECORD

Make a health folder for yourself. Every night this week, spend some time ferreting out your history of hospitalizations or major illnesses. Try to remember the years they occurred. The closer to the present year, the more accurate your list can be, listing names of doctors and places you were tested or treated. You may or may not choose to list regular check-ups.

Title your folder: Health History, _____ (your birthdate) _____ (the present year). This is pesty work if you're doing it for the first time, but once you've done it, adding to it is easy and you will always have a copy of your health history. You may choose to have two files within this folder: Old Health Histories, and Current Health History in this folder. Next, make yourself another folder entitled: Drugs, Supplements, and Vitamins. Create a file called: Past Drugs and Vitamins. Start as far back as you can, listing any drugs you have taken, the year, the prescribing doctor, and the reason. You may only be able to go back a year or so, but that's ok.

Make a second file: Drugs and Vitamins_____ (this year's date). List any and all drugs you take, the dosage, who prescribed them, and for what purpose. Organize the page into groups: Daily, As Needed, Temporary, Supplements. Each time something changes, make a new page for this file, listing the date at the top. Every time you visit a doctor you can print out two pages to hand them: one of your Health History and one of your Drugs and Vitamins_____ (this year's date). You will save *enormous* amounts of time and energy for your nurses, doctors, hospitals and yourself by doing so. You may also save your life, as occasionally drugs can interact with each other and be affected by supplements. Your goal for the month is to create a separate, easily accessible health folder for each member of your household. In the chaos of our constantly changing healthcare system, you will do well to be organized and in control of your own information.

NOT AS INTENDED

In your travels, you will have seen signs which do not convey their messages properly, due to spelling or punctuation errors. Sometimes, the sign has an unintended, secondary meaning. When you spot one of these, take a photo or write it down.

Compile a list of these signs. When you need a conversation starter, ask others about signs they have seen that are funny. Pretty soon, you will all be swapping humorous anecdotes about what you've seen.

MISTACKES
happen
EMBRACE
T   H   E   M

MORE THAN SHARING

The 2016 movie "Queen of Katwe" is based on the true story of a ten-year-old Ugandan girl who is given the opportunity to learn chess which helps her find a way to escape the overwhelming poverty of her surroundings.

Consider the activities you enjoy doing: skating, break dancing, concocting the perfect barbecue sauce, boatbuilding, beekeeping, tree pruning, or any skill you have. Call a school or library and offer to give a talk and a demonstration of your special skill.

Reach out to one of the many schools that lack funding. You may be opening a door to a whole new world for a young person.

MATTERS OF THE ARTS

Purchase several pads of 9 inch x 12 inch white drawing paper and as many sets of water-soluble markers as you can afford. Buy some packages of museum putty (available online). Call your local school and ask if they would like a volunteer to do an art project with the students.

Ask the kids to choose five of their favorite things, places or people to draw. Once they have chosen, tell them to pick one and make a drawing of it using the markers. Suggest that they leave space at the bottom to write a few sentences describing their picture and why they chose that topic. Have them sign it using their first names and their age. Ask the school, the students and their parents if you can display their artwork in your local library. Mount the art on pieces of foam board which will be mounted on the walls with museum putty. Write at the top of the foam board: ART MATTERS to the children of _____ (fill in the name of the neighborhood).

LEARN TO DEBATE

Find a friend who trusts you but with whom you disagree about something. Ask if they are willing to discuss the subject. Lay some ground rules: Each of you will make an opening statement about the topic, such as, "Climate change is man-made." The other person might state, "Climate change is cyclic; not man-made." This is just an example.

Your discussion can be about anything, from the profound to the banal, such as what to do on the weekend. Having prepared ahead of time, each person will have five minutes (use a timer) to present his/her argument. Ground rule: The other person must remain silent but may take notes. Then switch places. After both of you have presented your argument, you will take turns discussing the points the other person made.

Be respectful; if you disagree, write a note. Ground rule: *really* listen, rather than thinking about your next statement. Pay attention to each other's body language; are you getting angry, anxious…? Look the other person in the eye and nod to show you understand what they are saying. Use phrases like, "I can see what you are saying," or "Here's what I don't understand about what you just said."

Ground Rule: If either person presents something as a fact, they must provide sources to back up their opinion. While it is ok to feel a certain way, neither of you may say, "I just feel that way," without providing reasons.

Ground Rule: Set a finite time for your discussion to end. Ten minutes prior to the end, each person will take five minutes to sum up, stating their view. This should include any new ideas they have learned from the other person. If nothing has changed, something should be said such as, "Although we may continue to disagree over this topic, we agree over many other things. Thanks for helping me understand the way you think about this."

A PIECE OF YOUR MIND

Practice using the phrase, "What do you think?" Find three to five people today who are commenting on or complaining about an issue. Ask them, "What do you think?" Then be quiet and listen to their answer. If you are in a line, or somewhere where you are not likely to have a long conversation, their answer may be short. If you are at home or with someone who has more time to chat, ask them, "Why do you feel that way?" when they state their opinion. Note their responses.

Try this with people of all ages, sexes, and races, if possible. Others will be pleased that you care what they are thinking and that you are actually listening to them. In this way, you will be a more appealing person because you are learning to listen, and you will understand others better.

SAVORING

Buy several fresh navel oranges and squeeze the juice out into a jar. Find a wine glass or something thin and clear. Pour the fresh-squeezed juice into the glass. Hold the glass up in front of a window. Admire the color. Tip the glass a little and note how much the juice coats the glass. Hold the glass up to your nose. Inhale deeply to get a good whiff of the juice. Close your eyes and imagine the first sensations of taste: the initial sweetness, the sudden tart tang. Recall a time when you were parched from working outside; how dry and uncomfortable your mouth felt. Think how delicious orange juice would have tasted. Take a sip of your juice, holding it in your mouth for a moment before swallowing.

During World War II, oranges were scarce in America. They were regarded by some as an incredible, almost magical gift. Imagine yourself eating scraps of whatever you can scrounge; bread, potatoes, for what seems like ages. And then, by some miracle, you are given…an orange! Drinking the juice would be like swallowing sunlight. There are people right now in war-torn areas of the world; some are children. You can help get food to them by joining or supporting one of many reputable charities such as Feed the Children, The American Red Cross, or the International Rescue Committee. We have so much that we forget what joy an orange can bring.

LISTEN TO THEIR THOUGHTS

Strike up a conversation with a teenager you know well, either through family, friends, or your work. After chatting for a few minutes, ask this teen what they think about specific politicians or issues currently in the news. Be sure to listen carefully to their answers and refrain from interrupting. If they tell you what their parents think, gently say, "Actually, I'm really interested in what *you* think and why you think that." If they answer in short phrases, prompt them for more details. Whether their response is positive or negative, ask them why they hold this belief. Once again, pay close attention.

Wait until they are completely finished before responding. Then, you might ask, "So . . . what kind of a person do *you* want to be?" Listen without commenting. Lastly, ask them if they have a philosophy of life—a credo. You may have to explain what you mean and share your own credo. If they don't have a credo, finish up your chat with, "Thanks for talking with me. You're an interesting person and I hope you continue to develop your personal philosophy of life." If they ask you why that is important, say, "Because it's easier to find your way through life's challenges and joys with a map."

SILHOUETTE

Make a silhouette picture of someone. You need a dark room, a chair with a back, a bright, fixed light source even with the seated subject's head, a dark pencil, and a large sheet of white paper taped against the wall with low-tack tape, a sheet of black paper, larger than the person's head and a piece of white or light-colored illustration board to mount the silhouette on..

1. Seat the model so that their head casts a profile shadow on the wall on the white paper.

   The model must hold their head still while you trace the edge of their shadow on the paper, including their neck and part of the top of the shoulder, ending with the collar line.

2. Try to adjust the light so that the shadow is slightly smaller than the person's actual head, making sure you have a sharp shadow.

3. Once you have traced the shadow's outline, turn the lights on. Cut out the silhouette very carefully and use it as a pattern whose outline you will trace onto your black paper.

4. Finally, using small, sharp scissors or a swivel knife, cut out your silhouette. Spray the back with spray-mount and adhere it to the illustration board, carefully centering it. Have someone frame it professionally. Oval frames will work well.

IN IT TOGETHER

When you are in a waiting room of a hospital or medical office, look at the faces of fellow patients. If you see someone who looks frightened, bored, or is there alone, make eye contact and smile at them. If they return your smile and you are seated near them, strike up a conversation about something pleasant.

Most people are more than glad to be distracted. Talking with others can calm both of you. Regardless of our race, sex, or age group, when we face medical tests or procedures our superficial differences fall away, and we all become "just vulnerable humans."

PATIENCE

Are you always in a hurry to get things done? Are you annoyed by other people's pace if it differs from yours? When we rush, we miss things that are going on around us; for example, hurrying down the sidewalk means you are less likely to notice the colors of leaves overhead, a lovely garden, or a cat sunning itself in an apartment window.

You may not notice other people except to view them as objects in your way. Do you sigh and roll your eyes in the checkout line when the checker can't find the price of an item and has to look it up on a list? Do you honk your horn if the driver ahead hesitates a few seconds when the light turns green? Do you eat and drink faster than the people you are with, rather than savoring the flavors? Are you a person who frequently interrupts others or talks over them?

These habits can be reversed, but only if you are aware of them. Ask five people who know you well if they would describe your personality as: (a) slow-going, (b) mellow, (c) average, (d) nervous, (e) impatient, (f) angry, or (g) frantic. Ask them for particular examples of why they feel that way. If several people chose d, e, f, or g, you may wish to consider ways of calming yourself.

It is always a good idea to consult a professional, such as a social worker, a healthcare worker, or a spiritual leader to help you discover the sources of your behavior. Keep a daily journal in which you note each time you act impatiently. Do this for several weeks to find the situations which trigger your stress. Choose a phrase to repeat when you are stressed, such as "Slow down" or "Breathe deeply." Say these phrases slowly and pay attention to your breathing. Life goes by quickly enough; it is a shame to miss things by rushing through it.

CULLING

Do you attempt to do too much and end up frustrated and unsatisfied with yourself? Take out your notebook and make a list of everything you wish to accomplish today. Now add to the list all the things that you *should* accomplish. Make a third list, combining the two but ranking the tasks in order of importance. This will involve some executive decision-making.

Study this last list carefully. Realistically, how many of these things can you do today? Eliminate everything except the top three things you have decided are most important to you. Plan your day so that, no matter what, you accomplish those three things. Reward yourself by doing something you wanted to do from your first list.

Each day, do this exercise. If you find you have tons of time left over, add one more item from your third list. If you do this consistently, you will feel better about yourself, learn how much you can reasonably take on and accomplish and learn to cull things from your days that are not really important but take up your time so that you never finish anything.

SIMPLE GIFTS

Find a moment when you can be alone. It may be in your car, your home, the locker room, the woods, your bed, a bathroom, on the water, or in a crowd (Yes, it is quite possible to be alone in a crowd). Feel your body working: your heart beating, your lungs breathing, your throat swallowing. Feel the weight of your hands in your lap. Take pleasure in these things as you re-emerge into the world. Be grateful for your life.

HOLLOWNESS OF THE ARROGANT

Vanitas, vanitatum…Be wary of arrogant people. They have a false impression of their worth and importance. Like the wooden dolls one opens, only to find another wooden doll, which contains yet another, the self-important person often lacks substance. Rather than growing outwards, reaching towards others and the world, they hide within the shells they construct for protection, like a chambered nautilus.

In your travels, find a chambered nautilus shell or look one up. See how attractive they can be; how they shine like pearls. The human version, like the nautilus or the painted hollow doll, can be very captivating. Do not be deceived by appearances.

Arrogant, narcissistic people need to view others as inferior in order to support their own feelings of superiority. They create problems because of their divisiveness and leave others feeling inferior. Choose to associate with people who know themselves; their strengths and weaknesses and seek to create unity.

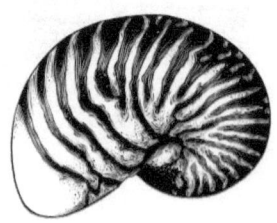

YOUR OWN PERSONAL VIEW

Go to an art store and buy a small sketchbook and some good lead drawing pencils: HBs (medium lead). You will need a gray kneaded eraser and a white plastic eraser. In your travels, when you see something that interests you, make a quick sketch of it.

For example, you might draw a crowd of people as a bunch of circles getting smaller and less detailed as they grow farther away. These drawings should have all the freedom of the scribble drawings you did as a kid. Try to draw what you see. For example, most people, when asked to draw a house, draw the same house! You know the one: it has a door in between two windows and chimney on the roof with smoke coils coming out.

Draw the basic shapes first, before you forget the details. Stick figures are fine, as are caricatures of your model. Look up the great writer, James Thurber's drawings. Even the lines he drew were funny. The idea is to draw whenever you're standing around somewhere; if you do it enough, you will invent your own short-hand; a signature style.

The next thing to do is when you hear something on the news that angers you, make a cartoon drawing of it. Your drawing is your own small world in which you are the creator. Illustrating the people and things that upset you robs them of their power in *your* world. Your pencil is your magic wand.

COGITATING AND PROJECTING

In the waning days of this year, write down five questions:

1. What was the best and worst thing that happened in the world this year?

2. What was the best and worst thing that happened to me, personally, this year?

3. What is my greatest hope for the world next year?

4. What is my greatest hope for me next year?

5. How will I help make number 3 and number 4 happen?

After you have answered the questions, carry your questions with you. Pose these five questions to people you know of all ages. Make a bunch of copies of the questions. Give a copy to each person who answers your questions.

ENJOYING NEW WORLDS

One of the best ways to bring people together from different cultures is through trying each other's cuisine. Choose a restaurant or food stand that features food from another culture. Make sure there are people from that culture who eat there. Once you are seated, look around until you see a dish that looks good. Ask the person serving you to tell you what the dish is called and what is in it. You may also ask the waitperson to help you decide on your food as they will know the most popular choices and should be familiar with the ingredients.

Once your meal arrives, eat slowly so as to fully appreciate the new flavors and textures. You may want to ask your server about specific ingredients you haven't experienced before. Sometimes, a person at another table will overhear you trying to figure out what to try. They may smile at you and suggest you try something next time. You may even end up chatting with them. If you live near an area that has stores that sell ingredients needed for the particular cuisine you are eating, follow up your meal by planning a visit to one of those markets. This is another excellent opportunity to explore new worlds, meet people, and expand your knowledge and appreciation of the wonderful diversity of human cuisine.

NO, NO NEGATIVES!

Listen to yourself today. Think about what you plan to say before you say it. Your goal is to go an entire day without saying anything negative. This may be harder than you imagine.

If you find yourself blurting out criticisms, ask yourself, "In what situations am I most likely to complain, whine, and criticize?" Write down your observations. Then you can work on preparing for those circumstances, one at a time. Of course, there are times in which it is appropriate to say negative things. But like seasoning, a little goes a long way.

FLYING HIGH

You are going to make a kite so you will be ready for spring. You will need a piece of lightweight but strong paper at least 36 by 36 inches, 2 thin tomato support stakes made of bamboo less than ¼ inch thick, a coping saw or mat knife, a roll of duct tape, a roll of packing tape, scissors, kite string and several yards of yarn. You will also need some material for a tail, as well as a partner, preferably someone young who has never made their own kite before.

1. Cut one of the sticks to measure 30 inches in length. Cut the other to measure 25 inches. Holding the longer stick vertically, make a mark 10 inches from the top. Mark the center of the 25-inch stick and place it at right angles to the other stick, matching the marks. With two thin pieces of duct tape, make an X at the join, securely taping the sticks together at right angles.

2. Tape the yarn to the top of the vertical stick with duct tape. pull the yarn to the tip of the horizontal stick on the right and tape, continuing on to the bottom stick and the tip of the stick on the right. Finish by taping the yarn to the top and clip. You should now have a diamond shape.

3. Lay your kite frame on the paper and carefully draw around the diamond adding 1 inch on each line. Remove your frame and fold the extra inches in toward you.

4. Before final assembly, you may wish to decorate your kite with paint or markers.

5. Lay the frame on the inside of the kite and tape the folds over the yarn with packaging tape. Tape the entire length of the yarn.

6. Now tie a piece of kite string a yard long around the middle X joint. Poke a hole through the kite and feed the other end of the string through it so it comes out on the front of the kite. Make a secure knot. You will tie your kite string to this.

7. Make a tail for your kite from light material about 3 inches wide and 6 feet long. Pass it in-between the button corner of the kite and the stick and tie it off.

While you wait for spring, scout out an open place to fly your kite. Choose somewhere away from overhead lines and tree branches. Parks, riverbanks, meadows, and beaches are good choices. Anchor your string on a stick or a fishing reel. If you can get other prospective kite makers involved, you can plan a kite festival/picnic. Once you have tested your kite and flown it a few times, you can send "notes" up the string, by cutting out small pieces of paper with a cut leading to a very small center hole. Slide the "note" onto the string so the string is at the center hole. The wind will carry the note upwards on the kite string. These are the perfect vehicles for wishes and prayers.

FLYING THE KITE.

EXAMINING HATE

Think of someone you dislike or hate. Open your journal to a blank page and make two columns. In the first column, list five qualities or behaviors this person displays that you dislike. In the second column, list five positive qualities or behaviors that you attribute to this person.

On the next page of your journal, list possible reasons for each of the person's good and bad qualities and behaviors. You may use your imagination for this part. Do you share any of the positive or negative qualities that you have listed? If so, consider how others may view you. Having done so, is there something you would like to change about yourself?

GET BACK TO ME

List the last five times you have needed a response from someone. This could be a call back from a doctor, a favor you have asked from someone, a response to a complaint about an order, confirmation of a date with a friend or family, or a question you need answered by someone before you can proceed with your task.

In a notebook make three columns. In the first column, write the name of the person or institution involved. In the second, list the result and how long it took for their response. In the third, write how the timing of the responses affected you.

We are all increasingly busy; social media takes up hours of our lives that used to be devoted to hobbies, exercise, and socializing. As a result, we have developed the idea that a prompt response is not necessary.

This serves us well when we are barraged by ads and requests from people unrelated to us. However, the next time someone asks you for information that they need to get on with their lives, remember this exercise and respond in a timely fashion.

THE COMFORT OF COCOA

Were you aware that hot chocolate used to be such a popular beverage that there were specially made hot chocolate pots and cups? It was considered a refined, sophisticated drink for adults.

With the advent of instant hot cocoa powder, hot chocolate has become a drink for children or for individuals in wintertime only. Yet, a cup of real cocoa is a comforting pick-me-up in any season.

1. Buy some "Dutched cocoa" powder. (This is cocoa that has been treated with an Alkalizing ingredient to reduce the bitterness). Assemble some honey, milk, half and half, and a dash of cayenne powder.

2. Heat half a cup of milk and ½ cup of half and a half per cup of cocoa. Do not let the milk come to a boil.

3. Add one to two heaping teaspoons of cocoa powder, one at a time. Stir until dissolved.

4. Slowly add the honey, one teaspoon at a time, to taste. You must keep stirring the cocoa all the while so the bottom of the pan does not scorch.

5. Take the smallest possible pinch of cayenne and stir it in. You may serve the cocoa in thick crockery mugs or delicate china cups.

6. Marshmallows are optional.

THE MAIN CAST

In your travels, look for an individual who is "wallpaper" in your world; someone whom you see fairly often but never speak with, such as the barista who makes your coffee, the sandwich truck person, the crossing guard at the corner...

Think about this person for a day. Who is their family and what are they like? What are their dreams for their future? What sorrows have they experienced? Do you like them? Imagine if they suddenly disappeared; would this impact your life?

Make up a little story about them and write it down. Finally, having explored your view of them, when you next see them, realize that they are yarn in the weave of your life. If you appreciate what they do, tell them so. Perhaps you will learn something about this individual which will change your understanding of them.

SET IN YOUR WAYS

Look up the phrase, "Confirmation Bias." This week, pay close attention to your own beliefs, especially the ones you are most emotional about. Ask yourself where your belief came from and then look into the facts regarding it. What would it take for you to change your belief? Can you accept new evidence that goes against what you have always thought?

Do you only feel good about yourself when your beliefs are considered correct? Feeling this way condemns us to either associate only with people just like us or to feel badly a great deal of the time when we are amongst others in the world.

Learning to adapt to new information, adjusting our opinions accordingly, is an important skill every living creature needs for survival, physically as well as emotionally. Reach out and expand your comfort zone.

NOBODY'S CHOICE

You are walking down the street or are stopped at a light in your car or in a subway car when you see someone begging. It makes you anxious. Some people have signs, stating their predicament. Some ask only for work, others for money. Some of us think, "Don't make eye contact. Why doesn't the government take care of these people? Why can't this person go to a shelter? If I give them money, they'll just buy drugs or alcohol with it."

Consider your own situation. Do you have savings? If you had a catastrophic event happen in your family, have you a backup plan or an extended family that would take you in? Anyone can become homeless; it is likely you have met people who were once homeless. If you wonder why people are reluctant to stay in shelters, volunteer at one for a week to see for yourself.

Has anyone dear to you ever had a mental problem, dementia, a substance abuse problem, lost their job, or shown up with unexplained bruises or broken bones? None of us are insulated from tragedy. If you are asked for money by someone where there are people nearby, smile at them and ask their name. Listen to what they have to say. If you feel safe and decide to offer someone cash, you must accept the idea that they may or may not use it for food. Instead, ask if they are hungry. If they are, you could choose to buy them a meal and a beverage. Homelessness is a complex problem with many causes. Rather than becoming infuriated, frightened or frustrated by our increasing homeless population, get involved. Call your town or city officials and ask what needs to happen to get people housed safely. You will sleep better at night.

COLD COMFORT

Carry extra tissues, the kind in the little plastic packs. When some-one nearby cannot stop coughing or sneezing, offer them a few tissues, saying, kindly, "I always carry extra tissues. May I give you a pack?"

Bring cough drops to share too; the individually wrapped kind. Nothing is more embarrassing than coughing in public and not be-ing able to stop. By helping someone to contain their germs you are not just helping that individual; you are protecting yourself and others in the area.

MODIFY YOUR BEHAVIOR

Identify a negative habit in yourself. Bad habits are like plantar warts, growing deeper with time, resulting in more and more pain. We cause ourselves much distress by rationalizing, rather than doing the hard work of fixing ourselves.

But take heart! Change is always possible and there are plenty of people willing to help. Make a plan; get started. Your level of anxiety may decrease just because you are taking action instead of being a passive victim.

If the habit you wish to eliminate is a dangerous one that could lead to injury to yourself or others, you need to consult a professional to get some help.

A COOL GATHERING

Hold an ice cream social. Find a group of ice-cream-loving friends and ask everyone to choose their favorite brand to contribute. A gallon or two quarts of each flavor is best if there are more than five attending the social. If you have fewer than five people coming, ask people to bring two quarts, each of a separate flavor. Make sure you have on hand coolers filled with ice in which to sink the tubs of ice cream. You will need scoops, bowls, spoons and lots of napkins, and clean-up equipment. Access to running water is helpful. Supply several pitchers of clean water for rinsing bowls in-between flavors.

Nice to have but not essential: sprinkles, finely chopped nuts, sliced bananas, strawberries, peaches, or coconut. Hint: make sure you stage this in a place with plenty of shade. Holding your social at lunchtime helps avoid the afternoon heat and the bees. Keep extra bags of ice so that coolers can be refilled to take home any uneaten ice cream.

HUNGER

Take a day where you will not be required to do any heavy work or anything physical. Decide to set this day aside to skip a meal or two. Check first with your primary care physician first to ask if this will be safe for you and if so, how many meals are safe for you to skip. Then see that you stay hydrated by drinking water in the morning and throughout the day.

Go about your business without telling people that you are fasting. Take some notes about the way your body responds to going without food. The next morning, resume eating, savoring each taste, temperature and texture.

Return to your normal pattern of eating with the awareness of what it feels like for a healthy well-fed adult to feel hunger, if only for a short period.

UNKNOWN WORLDS

Take an art adventure. Go online and locate the art museum that is nearest you. This could be as large as The Met or The Louvre or as small as a gallery that has American, European, African, Asian, or Native American art. If you have nothing at all nearby, go to the library and pick out several art history books. Spend several hours or more looking at the pictures or the sculptures. Many museums have on-line tours.

In your notebook, record any particular style, period, or artist you find intriguing, exciting, confusing, or aggravating. List all the information you can about the works you have identified in each category. On your next foray into art, look at your list and spend some time pouring over each style, period, or artist on your list. Perhaps, you are drawn to both Greek mosaics and the art of the Plains Indians. What are the things about each that you like? Are there any similarities between these two styles?

Look back at your list. Were you confused by Cubism? Look it up. Why would anyone start seeing the world this way? What were the artists who began Cubism influenced by? Now, if you hated some styles or works of art, identify why you felt that way. Do you think the artist meant to disturb or jar the viewer? Finally, in this art adventure, choose one artist to look up. Find out who they were, where they lived, how they learned their craft, and who their friends were. What was the world like when they were alive? What is it you like about their work? Can you imagine yourself as their friend, student, lover, or teacher? What would that be like? Return from your adventure refreshed and enlightened. You will start noticing the visual world in a different way from before.

SIMPLE AND SANITARY

Note how often you or others put your fingers in your mouth. Go to the drug store and purchase several small manicure kits which have nail files and scissors packed up in a plastic case. Keep one in the glove compartment of your car and another at your home.

Having files and manicure scissors will eliminate trying to nip cuticles or nail snags with your teeth. Using teeth never works, usually making things much worse. It often tears the skin and or causes you to put your fingers in your mouth all the more, exposing yourself to germs.

You have the power to protect your health by simply taking care of your hands.

V.I.Hs

If you are feeling powerless, lonely, anxious, or depressed, visit your local animal shelter and ask to help. Volunteering to spend some time walking a dog or paying some attention to one of the cats or dogs will empower you. These creatures are homeless by no fault of their own. Walking, petting, grooming, or feeding a lonely creature makes you a Very Important Human.

Making any life a little better is a worthwhile endeavor that gives one purpose and satisfaction.

LOVE KNOTS

Learn to braid. Braiding is a useful skill for anyone who works with hair, rope, decorative knotwork or jewelry. The best way to start is to find an illustrated book with clear pictures broken down into steps. The 1995 Klutz book "Hair, A Book of Braiding and Styles" by Anne Johnson, has many examples for people with straight or curly hair that is longish. If your hair grows in tight curls or has good body, you may like "The Hair Braid It Manual" by Afiya Hopson. This book has instructions for both long and short styles using braiding techniques.

If you are trying to learn to braid rope, you could start with "Basic Knots and Ropework," by Vince Brennan. These are just a few examples of braiding and knot-tying books and tutorials available. Once you learn to braid, you can teach your kids. Working with one's hands develops fine motor skills while stimulating the brain.

Braiding is a craft that can be taken with you, requiring few supplies or space. Braiding's close relatives, knitting and crocheting, are recommended by the Anxiety Resource Center. Repetitive movement of the hands distracts the brain from worries, teaching our brains to focus.

INSPIRATION GENTLY GIVEN

On a small piece of paper, write in a ballpoint pen: "Do good to-day." Fold it up carefully. (If you can fold it into an interesting shape, like a simple origami, all the better). On the outside, print neatly, "Open me." Leave your note where someone is sure to find it, either in public or at home. Make sure it can't blow away and become litter.

OLFACTORY SKILL

Choose three dishes you really enjoy but have never cooked yourself. In your journal, write the name of each dish at the top of a page. Now, try to identify the ingredients in the columns below, listing the obvious first. For example, let's use macaroni and cheese, which hails from the colonial period in America. (Its invention is attributed to James Hemmings, an enslaved person of color who was trained in French cooking and was Thomas Jefferson's chief cook).

The first thing to notice when tasting this dish is that it includes pasta in a cheese sauce. Because the sauce is thickened, we may assume it would be made with milk and flour. But what other tastes can you observe: onions…garlic? Do you taste any other flavorings, such as Worcestershire sauce? There are many ways to alter Hemming's original recipe, so you may encounter other ingredients, depending upon the version you follow.

Now think of a home-made dish you enjoyed as a child. Can you name the ingredients involved? Today, many of us live on a diet of fast food, which is full of fat, sugar and preservatives. We have forgotten how to savor foods that don't consist of hamburgers, french fries, and soda. If no one cooked in your family, you can begin a healthier tradition. Nutritious great-tasting food does not have to be expensive to make or complicated. This exercise will sharpen your appreciation for what you are eating, which will help you to make healthier choices. The dishes you choose for this assignment can be simple pasta dishes made with three or four ingredients, vegetable dishes, complex stews or stir-fries. We are born with the great gift of our senses. The more we educate and exercise them, the more we enjoy having them.

THE CENTER OF YOUR UNIVERSE

As you go about your sphere of activities, think about the meaning of that word, "sphere." Today we think of a sphere as an object in which every point is equidistant from the center.

Aristotle taught that the earth was the center of a system of concentric crystal spheres which contained the stars and heavenly bodies. Certain individuals feel that they are the center of the universe, with the people closest to them being the most important. The farther away other people, nations, and problems are from themselves, the less attention and care they spend on them.

Consider your own sphere of influence and that of your country. Do you believe everything revolves around you and yours? Come up with a better system of thinking about how we influence one another, each other's countries, the planet. Do some drawings if you find that helpful. Ask your friends and families to puzzle this out with you.

IN THE FULLNESS OF TIME

Decide that today you are going to do a superior job at whatever you do. Pick something out of your day you would normally do on automatic pilot. Focus on it, identifying the components of the task. For example, if you are cooking, make something from scratch. This doesn't have to be complicated or time-consuming.

If you are at your office, decide to clean your desk and get a fresh start on today's task. If you go to a meeting, pay attention. Take notes. If you are a nurse, doctor, or teacher, do something extra for your class or patient to help or cheer them. Go out of your way to make their day special.

If you are an artisan or a builder, pay attention to detail. Whatever it is that you do, commit yourself to focus and not allow extraneous worries to plague you.

WHO COULD I BE?

Make up a fantasy family tree for yourself. You may or may not be familiar with your actual family tree; no matter. *This* family tree is pure imagination. First, choose your father and mother. Write their names, birthdays. If, in your fantasy, they are dead, include the dates they died. If married, write down their marriage date. Use a separate page for each person where you will describe their birthplace, family, and their work.

Add any interesting details you like. Be creative. When you finish, make up your maternal and paternal grandparents and write a page for each of them. Continue on with other family members or decide to develop one character or more in depth.

This is a fun exercise to do with other people you know. You may work on it over a period of time, then share your fantasy family history. When you are finished, ask yourself what strengths and weaknesses you gave your family. Were they similar to your real-life family?

Ask yourself why you chose these particular characters. For example, were they famous, rich, nefarious, honest, kind...? Keep these "family members" and add to their stories. You may end up with a novel!

IN ORDER OF IMPORTANCE

Take a little trip this week. It can be somewhere new or a favorite haunt. The trip can be short, as in a lunch hour, or as long as you can afford. The purpose is to give you time away from your everyday environment to consider what matters most in your life.

List at least three things that are important to you. Then determine what is necessary for them to exist. For example, you might list a spouse or a child. Then, you might decide that they require a stable home with heat, food, and clean water.

Next, ask yourself what you need in order to have that home, food, and water. For example, you might say you need an income to provide these things. Spend some time deciding what is really needed in your life. You should return from your trip with a list of priorities for your life to be happy.

I SUBMIT

Consider the word, "submit." It can mean "to present for consideration" or "to surrender." Most people who work will, at some time, have to submit proposals of one type or another: lesson plans, dissertations, resumes, business campaigns, and scientific discoveries. Painters, dancers, choreographers, musicians, writers, sculptors, and actors all have to present themselves or their work for consideration continually and must learn to develop tough hides. Many times, if not most of the time, they get passed over or their work gets rejected.

Regardless of our field of work, all of us need to learn not to take rejection personally. In your travels, consider how often you "submit" yourself or your work to others (your boss, your clients, your family, the public). Do your best and learn to develop a thick skin.

Ask yourself if you "surrender" by being hurt, or giving up when others reject you, your work, or your ideas. Listen carefully to others' critiques, but remember, they are subjective. Learn from them, make changes if the critique is fair and move on.

ONE-DAY WONDER

This weekend, choose a small project that you would normally try to complete within a day. Divide it into four parts. Schedule your day so that two of the parts can be completed on the first day with time left over to do other things. You may do both of the two parts in the morning or the afternoon or you may break them up, doing one-quarter of the project in each. Do the same with the other two parts the following day.

Your project should be a small one; something that you can easily finish in the time you allotted. The point is to learn to structure yourself so that you succeed at accomplishing tasks without stress. Some of us have never been taught how to discipline ourselves and create reasonable schedules. Completing tasks helps us develop self-trust. Simply saying, "Oh, I'm really bad at…. (cleaning, practicing, responding to people, keeping promises)" sets you up for failure and a chaotic, stressful lifestyle. Take charge of your time. Once you can accomplish small projects, trusting yourself to follow through, you can take on larger goals.

GAINING YOUR WINGS

If you live where there is snow, once it snows, go to a public sledding hill and ask some parents and their kids if anyone knows how to make a snow angel. The kids will most likely want to help. Ask them to demonstrate. Then try one yourself.

Gather a group of friends of all ages to make snow angels outside of a hospital or nursing home where people looking out the windows can see them.

TRICKSTERS

On April Fool's Day, gently trick a family dinner guest. Gather some small flat pebbles about the size of a dry lentil (or use a dry lentil). Place one under each cereal or soup dish at your family's table. They should rock the bowl just slightly; not enough to spill the liquid within, or find the perfect brown stone that looks like a large, uncut potato, one that won't fit in a soup spoon or a person's mouth. Clean and sterilize it. Let everyone but the guest in on the joke. Serve homemade vegetable soup for the first course; something with potatoes in it. Place the stone in the guest's bowl along with the soup and watch what happens when the guest's spoon hits the rock. The weight of it will tip off your guest long before it reaches their mouth.

The oldest person or the youngest in the family may be the "trickster" who places the stone in the Stone Soup. These tricks delighted generations of families, creating stories that were retold at family gatherings to everyone's delight.

THE MAGICAL SOCK

Make a sock puppet. Collect all of the socks whose mates have run off to wherever missing socks go and choose one. You will need some red or pink material, 4 inches by 8 inches, a fabric marking pencil you can see against the pink and red, sewing scissors, a piece of cardboard 8 inches by 10 inches, an iron and board, needle, thread, sewing pins, colored felt for mane and tail, and buttons for eyes.

1. Put your hand inside the sock with your fingers together at the toe and your thumb in the heel part. Touch them together, folding the toe towards the heel with your thumb touching your index finger. The sock will look like a snake with a mouth.

2. Trace a mouth with the top line curving around the outline of the fingers like an upside-down U, beginning and ending where the fingers join the palm. Cut this line and fold the flap down, then trace and cut along it, mirroring the line of the top. The piece you have cut out should look like a stretched oval.

3. Remove the sock from your hand. Open the "mouth" on a piece of cardboard, holding the sock at a right angle to the table. Trace the mouth hole on the cardboard. Now, take the pattern and add ½ inch all the way around it.

4. Fold your red or pink fabric in half. Cut out the cardboard pattern and place it atop your pink or red material. Trace the outline with your marker, then cut out the fabric along the outline.

5. Hand or machine stitch the two pieces ½ inch from the outside edge, leaving one curve unstitched. Now, trim away ¼ inch from the edge. Clip both curved edges from the outside edge towards the stitching an eighth of an inch apart. Turn the oval inside-out and press, folding under the unstitched edge lines.

6. Mark your cardboard pattern with a line halfway across. Fold the cardboard on this line. If it is very stiff, you may score it lightly with a matte knife. Stuff the pattern inside your oval and stitch the open end closed.

7. Turn your sock inside-out and pin the edges of the pink or red oval to the *outside* edge of the mouth opening in the sock. Hand stitch it, removing the pins, and avoiding the cardboard. Turn the sock right-side out. Put your hand inside the sock.

8. Make your puppet into a dragon or a horse by sewing mane on the back and teeth or a tongue inside. You may use button eyes or make felt eyes and nostrils. If you prefer a soft mouth, don't insert the cardboard pattern in between the pink pieces.

9. Your puppet can be a person, a bunny, a cat, a dog . . . you choose. Now, let's get a whole group of people to do this so that we produce hundreds of toys and find a way to send them to refugee kids who have so little magic in their lives.

PLEASE, SIT

In your travels on public transportation or in waiting rooms, etc. look around you to see who needs a seat more than you, regardless of their sex or age. Offer to give them yours, regardless of your own sex or age.

SOLIDITY OF LIFE

"The Best remedy for those who are afraid, lonely or unhappy is to go outside, somewhere they can be quiet, alone with the heavens, nature and God. Because only then does one feel that all is as it should be." Anne Frank, 1929-1945. Anne wrote these words while in hiding, prior to being discovered by the Nazis and transported to the death camps, where she died. We who may or may not be in hiding from forces that would destroy us, need to take this young girl's wise advice.

Anxiety and despair thrive on separation from our fellow creatures. Hiding alone, indoors, our minds often ruminate over negative thoughts and depressing items in the news.

Go outside the next time the sky is blue and lovely. Sit somewhere and tip your face up so that the sun hits it. Close your eyes. Make a list, mentally or physically, of all the good sensations your body is experiencing; the way the wind sounds, the fragrance of the earth, the water, someone cooking. We have control over what goes forth from our own fragile bodies.

What we create becomes part of the layers of life that wrap our planet and everything in it. Realize that the choices we make are like the growth rings of a tree. Every life is part of the warp and weft of our beautiful planet.

DESPERATELY SEEKING SCIENCE

Visit a science museum. Take someone with you who has never visited one before. Most museums provide wheelchairs for those who use them. If you have a friend who is a veteran, call ahead to see whether they have special prices for vets.

If you live near Washington, D.C., the Smithsonian has a lot to offer. The National Museum of Space and Aeronautics is fascinating in and of itself, but all the more so to anyone who has ever flown a plane.

For children, a visit to a children's science museum can be thrilling and inspiring. Take notes of the things your guest is especially interested in. Then, when you go home, you can follow up on those topics. If you have gone with your child, ask them to tell you what they liked best and why.

FILLING THE NEED

Buy a small potted tulip or daffodil (or whatever spring flower will grow in your region). Once the frost has passed, on that first day when the sun warms the earth so that you can smell the rich soil, go to a park or a safe open space where there is no traffic threat. Take along the plant, a little bottle of water, a trowel, and a small child. (Be sure to get parental permission if the child is not your own). Ask them to look for a place that needs a flower. Don't do this in a manicured area; find an untended place that is not likely to be mowed. Help the child dig a hole and plant their flower and give it water. Stand back and admire it. Tell the child, "You have made this place look happier."

UNDER YOUR SKIN

In your travels, you may at some time develop a rash. Rashes can be caused by lots of things and most of them go away and are nothing to worry about. Many people get various reactions to plants like poison ivy, oak, or sumac. Other people get contact dermatitis from chemicals or dirt. Hives, ringworm, and sensitivity to insect bites can create itchy skin problems as well.

If you develop an inflammation that won't go away on its own, seek medical help before it becomes infected. In the same manner, small problems in life should be dealt with before they develop into full-blown catastrophes. Professionals with expertise should be consulted and, like a rash, the problem should be diagnosed, and cleansed. The source of the problem must be addressed to prevent a relapse.

When we allow problems to fester, we pay a high price in the end.

IN GRATITUDE

Pay attention to the people around you, whether in public or at home. Take note of any little act of kindness, tolerance, or courage that someone exhibits. This person can be any age. Go to that person and tell them you noticed that they did a good thing just then. Give them a smile and a "thumbs up."

MODERN DAY SCROOGES

Look up the word, "misanthrope." Have you become one? Look around at your friends, family, and elected officials and list those who have become misanthropes. Spring, for some religions, is a season where sacrifice plays a central role. While "sacrifice" can mean a ritualized killing of an animal or person as an offering to a god, there is another definition relevant to today. In modern societies, sacrificing has come to mean giving up something one values for the sake of someone else. People who do this are known as humanitarians.

Look again at those friends, family, and governmental officials who have become misanthropes. Are you a part of that group? Now imagine a group of humanitarians; people willing to sacrifice something; money, comfort, security, an idea long-held, perhaps even their own lives, for the good of others or the future of the planet. What would it take for the misanthropes to become more like the humanitarians?

SAVING GRACE

Recall at least three times when you were saved by someone or something. These could be situations where you were completely innocent of what was about to befall you or where you did something so thoughtless or mean that you deserved fate to come kick you in the butt; yet you were spared.

Go somewhere with your notebook where you can be alone and think over each of the three situations. Describe each situation in a few lines, such as: I cheated at work, but my boss gave me another chance, I shoplifted fruit from the grocer but my friend saw me and made me put it back, or, I drove drunk and nearly ran through a red light, but a cop pulled me over.

Below each incident description, write a few comments about why you did this, and who or what saved you from your mistake becoming much worse. Lastly, explain what you did to express your relief or gratitude towards the person, fate or higher power that intervened. If you have not thanked them, remember that you may still do so.

In your travels, be aware of others you might deter from making a mistake. Would you intervene, even if it entails personal discomfort, to spare someone harm, or embarrassment or worse? Can you pass on the grace that you, yourself have received?

THE SOUND OF ONE'S OWN VOICE

Look up the word, "adamant." List ten people to whom this word applies. Look up the word, "soliloquy." Compile a list of ten people who often speak in soliloquies. Are any of them the same people as those on your "adamant" list?

Now, look up "colloquy." Imagine some of the people on your two lists in a room at the same time. What would it take for them to have a colloquy about a controversial topic? Imagine yourself as the moderator in the room. What would you say? Lastly, see if your name belongs on either of the two lists.

ANTICIPATION

List four things you are eagerly anticipating. Place them in order of importance, with the most important first. Ask yourself the likelihood of each happening. Write under each how its occurring would improve your life. Now list how the failure of this important thing happening would alter your life.

Looking back at your worksheet, write two little stories, envisioning what the changes would lead to in both instances. Lastly, looking at the two stories you have written, write two more scenarios describing how the changes in your life (or lack thereof) affect your environment, both human and otherwise.

DEADLY TEMPTATIONS

Raisins, grapes, onions, garlic, corn cobs, chocolate, chewing or bubble gum containing Xylitol, an artificial sweetener, can harm or kill a dog or cat. If you have pets or have visitors with dogs or cats, do not have these objects around at all. Explain how these things can injure an animal. Never allow children or strangers to feed pets unsupervised.

Always have the number of a local animal hospital at hand, right next to the poison control number you have for humans. If you walk your dog, don't let them eat anything (like gum) someone left on the sidewalk. Don't carry gum in your own purse or pack, as dogs and cats can be tempted. Go online to research further, as animal nutritionists know a great deal about the nutritional needs of our pets.

Don't give them alcohol, cannabis, caffeine or nuts. Never allow your kitty milk or raw fish. Don't use needles or pins around pets as they can drop to the floor and be swallowed by pets. Look up poisonous plants. The list is long but includes some common houseplants and seasonal plants like Amaryllis bulbs, lilies, and Poinsettia. Give away the avocado tree you grew from seed. Do some research; you may save a life.

Collie.

GONE BUT NOT FORGOTTEN

American cemeteries didn't always exist. Read Keith Eggner's "Cemeteries" for the history of public graveyards. People were buried at home in small family plots. After the 1830's, graveyards began to be developed, eventually becoming large tracts of elaborately groomed landscaped ground full of beautiful sculptures. Since there were not yet public gardens or parks, people used cemeteries for picnics, recreation, and carriage rides. They were good places to be alone with your thoughts.

With this in mind, take a walk around a graveyard. Think over your life and identify one thing that you tried that failed. This can be anything, such as baking a cake from scratch, learning to speak Spanish, getting elected to a town office, finishing a degree, writing a song, being a good example to a child; whatever you wish that you had achieved.

Look around you at all the graves of those who have gone on and think about the many things those people may have accomplished. Sit down in the shade and consider what you have *succeeded* in doing. Pick one particular name out of all the graves; one that you find appealing for whatever reason. Addressing this person by name, tell them a little bit about yourself and the one thing you tried to do which failed.

Consider that all of us attempt and fail at many things, but the person you are addressing cannot try to succeed anymore. Tell them that you will keep trying because, being alive, you can start over. Explain what it is that you are going to attempt. Tell your silent friend that you may fail again, but you haven't given up. Consider how you will attempt to achieve your goal differently this time. You may come back as often as you need to. Make a good plan. This is the season of new beginnings. How will you start over?

USING YOUR SENSES

Take your journal on a sensory hunt. Choose an environment, such as an indoor location (a school, library, museum, theater, store, religious institution, jail) or an outdoor one. Spend at least an hour exploring your location with all your senses.

Choose words that will describe your hunt to someone else without your writing complete sentences. Go through each sense. What is the light like? Is the air dry or humid? What about the temperature? What noises are there? Describe any odors, good or bad. What are the textures like? If you stick out your tongue, how does the air taste?

Write the words that have come to you. Look them over. Without mentioning the location by name, would someone get a clear picture of where you were just from your list? Read the list to several people. Then ask them to try to guess your hunting grounds as clearly as they can.

FINDING YOUR RELATIVES

"Find your relatives." This is a phrase that was told to me when I was a painter. It means, to look for others creating work that relates to yours. Then study the work. The same advice could be applied to trying to improve in any field or in life. The experience of others with similar problems/goals can be extremely helpful to us in many ways, providing information and ideas which you might not have conceived of.

If you are having a particular problem, it pays to get help; but the trick is to get the *right* help. One way to do this is to talk with many people, try out their ideas and see what works or doesn't. You will have false starts and disappointments and dead ends. Keep talking and putting yourself out there.

If you are persistent and determined in your quest, you will eventually meet people who will introduce you to others who are pursuing similar objectives. These are your "relatives." Don't go it alone; you've got family!

ANONYMOUS PRAISE

On five small pieces of paper (any paper will do, but origami paper which you can buy at an art store is nicer) write or print neatly, preferably in ink, "Your goodness is an example to others." Choose five hard working, kind people whom you know deserve a lift or some joy in their lives.

Whenever you can without being noticed, post the notes where they will find them: on a desk, in their locker, through a mail slot, or you could just hand it to them. This might be the only acknowledgement they get. You may or may not choose to sign it. Everyone loves knowing they are admired and appreciated.

VISION QUEST

When you are driving in the rain, look around you at the cars; those going in the same direction as you and those traveling in the opposite direction. Have someone in the passenger seat take notes for you. Decide which cars are easiest to see in the early morning, daylight, evening, and night driving.

Pay attention to the car's color, its value (lightness or darkness), and, especially, whether or not it has its lights on. Ask your passenger to make a list, going from the easiest to see in bad visibility to the most difficult.

Repeat this exercise in snow, fog, and tunnels. Share your results with your friends and family. Based upon what you have learned, act accordingly when you drive, remembering that your lights should be on whenever you are using your wipers.

MOLDING THE FUTURE

On Earth Day, picture a young person you care about. This can be a relative, a friend, or someone you work with. Now think about an area that was natural and unspoiled when you were growing up which is now lost to over-development, lack of proper land or water management, or pollution.

Locate a different area which is still a healthy part of the earth, with clear skies, wildlife habitat, and clean water. Dedicate yourself to helping preserve it for the younger person you have chosen. Find out if there is an association with similar interests you may join. If you live in a city, petition the mayor for a community garden or green space for the community. Knock on doors and tell neighbors what it is you are trying to do and why. Ask them to come with you to meet with the mayor. Have a group meeting first to agree on a possible location. Call or visit other successful community garden groups for ideas. Planting indigenous trees in areas where they can safely thrive will help to filter the air, making the future brighter for the young person you have chosen.

THE PAUSE THAT REPLENISHES

Plan a nap. Some of us haven't had a nap since kindergarten. Don't worry if you can't doze off. Closing your eyes and lying down in a place with a comfortable temperature, cover yourself with a sweater or jacket if needed. If you can't lie down at work on your lunch break, sit back in a comfortable chair and elevate your feet.

Set a quiet alarm for fifteen minutes which should wake you, but not startle you. If the room is too bright or you are outside, buy a soft travel blindfold. Now, tell yourself that for fifteen minutes, you will not muse over problems, worries, illness, or anxieties.

If napping causes difficulty in sleeping at night, shorten the nap to ten minutes. You will awaken refreshed, and your mind will function better, especially if you are a worrier.

OUT OF THE ORDINARY

Take a trip to a flea market, a junk shop, a yard sale, or an antique store. Bring your family or some friends along, particularly if you have a few kids in the group. Have each person pick out an object and either take notes, a photo, or sketch it. If there are only a few people in your group, choose two or three objects each.

Now go home or somewhere where you can all sit and write down everything you can about your objects: How old are they? What shape are they in? Do they look used? How big are they? What are they made from? What colors are they? Looking at what you have written, decide on a character who would have owned or used the objects. Next, read what you have come up with for your group. These will be the main and supporting characters in a play.

Decide what kind of a play you wish to write: comedy, mystery, drama, or (for energetic groups) a musical. Brainstorm together and come up with a plot. Next figure out the relationships of the characters. Make up a rough outline of the story. When all is in place, begin writing the script.

Depending on the ages and number of people in your group, this can be an afternoon or a once-a-week activity. Your goal is to come up with an original play in which everyone has contributed to its creation.

RASCALS AND SCALLYWAGS

The word impeach, seen frequently in the news, is often misunderstood. It comes from the Latin, "impedicare," to entangle or catch. The word can be used to mean challenge or call into question. *Merriam-Webster* defines it: "to charge a (public official) before a competent tribunal with misconduct in office."

Decide what you think the parameters should be for impeachment. Make a list of ten people who lived during your life whom you think deserve impeachment. These do not have to be governmental officials for the purpose of this task. Place them in order of severity of their offenses. Then, for each, list the effects their behavior has had upon others. Lastly, ask ten people for their definition of impeach.

If we are to feel in control of our culture and society, we need to understand words that are tossed about and what they mean to us.

THE SOUND OF SILENCE

Buy a pair of ear plugs. Place an earplug gently in each ear, blocking the openings. Be careful not to stuff them too far into the opening. The idea is to seal your ears, so you don't hear sound clearly.

Have a partner test what you can hear by speaking to you from varying distances. If you can't hear anything at all, pull the earplugs out a bit. Spend some time experiencing your newly reduced hearing. It's best to try this at home with friends or family for a few hours. Do not do this outdoors or in dangerous situations such as driving.

The idea is to see what it is like asking people to repeat what they say, misunderstanding conversations, or having difficulty communicating due to hearing loss. Once you have experienced this for a day, you are less likely to be impatient around the folk who may not hear as well as you.

GET A GRIP

If you live where there is snow, keep your eye out for anyone having difficulty negotiating the sidewalks. (Make sure you have sturdy boots or crampons yourself). If you see someone struggling, offer them your arm and help them arrive at a place of safety. Even in the South, people may face deadly black ice. Take precautions so that you won't fall yourself. Then you will be able to help others.

OUR FELLOW ANIMALS

Visit your fellow animals. Go to a zoo or a nature preserve. If you don't have either near you visit a farm or a pet store. Bring your notebook. Make a list of animals, organizing them according to their locomotion: two-footed, four-footed, two-footed plus hands or tail, four-footed plus tail (amphibians) fins and tail...etc. For each group, write down each one's basic needs. List the foods (plants, meat, insects, fish, fruit) each group eats, indicating that food's source. What do they drink; where do they get it? Finally, find out the basic temperature required for each animal (including water temperature range needed by fish, reptiles and amphibians).

Spend some time admiring our fellow earthlings. Note that each creature has exactly what it needs to live: skin, coat, teeth, claws, hooves, gills, camouflage, night vision, or wings. Go home and consider how interdependent all species are. Being cut off from nature is unhealthy for us. Make sure you educate your children by introducing them to the earths' creatures. Knowing that other animals love their lives as much as humans do makes us more aware of our responsibilities to maintain a healthy ecosystem.

FINDING PEN PALS

If you are a member of a group: religious, educational, musical, sports, medical, etc., talk to your members about forming a pen pal association. The idea is to find a group of Americans located in a different part of the country with whom you can correspond.

Make sure your correspondents live in an area unlike yours. You can locate such a group by finding branches of your own association. Contact their leader and propose your idea. Establish ground rules to which both groups will adhere. Start off with each pen pal composing a little bio. You may choose to include photos or not. Talk about your cultures, your families, your favorite foods, and your environment. Describe a typical week in your area.

The purpose is to find out what you have in common and to make a connection with someone who experiences a different reality from yours.

PUT ON A HAPPY FACE

Take a walk through your town or a place where you feel comfortable. Walk past several strangers noting how many people offer you a smile. Now, offer your own friendly smile to passers-by. Note how many return it.

You don't have to be intrusive with your smiling experiment; there are places where people prefer to be left to their own thoughts, such as on public transport.

Think about how you feel when people return your smile. Realize that your smile brightens people's day and vice versa.

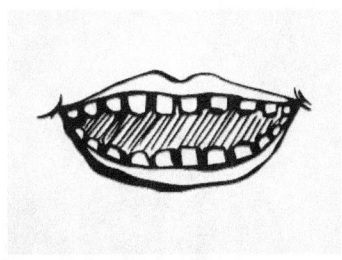

GROWING YOUR OWN

Plant a kitchen garden. It doesn't matter whether you have a patch of earth or not. Some of us live in apartments where our gardens grow in pots hanging from fire escapes or sit on windowsills or rooftops. Start with basic useful herbs: chives, cilantro, mint, thyme, oregano, or maybe tarragon. If you haven't grown things before, go to a garden center and ask for help. If you don't have access to sunlight, there are grow lamps that will allow you to grow plants indoors. If you have a child, they'll love growing something they can eat. Take a trip to a farm, if possible. Some farms allow visitors to stay over and assist with the chores.

It is important that we never forget that we are of the earth. We should pass this on to a generation that is often overly absorbed in the man-made technological world.

YIELDING THE WAY

When did you take your driving test? For many of us, it was long ago. Look up the rules of the road in your state. You can call the Department of Motor Vehicles and ask for a rule book or access the information online.

Most of us could use a refresher course, especially when it comes to yielding the right-of-way. When you drive to an intersection without a stoplight and arrive at the same time as another car opposite you, allow the car opposite to turn first. Make sure they see that you are waving them on with your hand.

When someone yields the right of way for you, thank them with a wave. If you see someone in another car behave graciously towards someone, give them a "thumbs-up." We're safer on the road if we pay attention and help each other get where we're going.

AWARENESS OF AIR

Take a walk in the sun. Bring along something yummy to eat and drink and a blanket. Carry a small journal and pencil. Find a grassy place to lie down after your snack. Feel the air around you, pressing against your skin. The air is not just an absence of *stuff* but is a thing unto itself.

Lie on your back and look up, facing the sky. Look through the air and notice how it filters what you see. Is it dry, wet, clear, or smoggy? Watch any clouds which may pass by for at least fifteen minutes. Write down any words or phrases which come into your mind and save them for later. They are seeds for stories, poems, and conversations.

If you dread making small talk, use this experience. Say something like, "You know, I was lying on my back in the grass the other day and I realized (or saw, smelled, overheard, felt) the most interesting thing." This is a great way to engage listeners.

IT'S EVERYBODY'S BUSINESS

Do you drink or use recreational drugs every day? See what happens when you skip a day or two. If you become obsessed with thoughts of what you are missing, consider filling your life with more challenges. If you can't have fun without drugs or alcohol, it is time to get professional help in cutting back.

Ask your kids if your use of recreational drugs or alcohol troubles them. Loud parties where friends or you get smashed or stoned and act abnormally are alarming to young children who depend upon you. You are also providing a model for future behavior. Kids may not be able to verbalize their concerns, so you need to have a heart-to-heart with them. Ask them, "When Mommy and Daddy have drinks that you can't have or when we smoke pot do you think we act silly? How does that make you feel? Does it ever scare you?" Then listen actively to their response.

If you are acting responsibly, there usually won't be a problem. But if you drink every night and then fight, you need to stop doing both, as you are harming your children and setting them up for troubled futures. We all must make responsible choices as well as sacrifices for those we love. This is the essence of teaching healthy love (including self-love) to your kids, without which they cannot grow up to care about the welfare of themselves, you or others.

THE COST OF THAT CUP

Instead of spending five or six dollars on a coffee drink that has hundreds of calories and lots of sugar, buy a cup of regular coffee or make your own at home. Then, collect the money you would have spent on coffee that week and visit a good second-hand store where you can purchase items inexpensively. At seasonal changes, you may be able to buy cartons of winter or summer clothes for next to nothing.

Store the items until next fall, when homeless shelters, safe houses, churches, synagogues, and mosques which help the poor will be needing these items. Similarly, at the end of summer, pick up sandals, bathing suits, and summer clothes to help out the following year. Bring your children with you to hunt for the good stuff. It will become one of their best memories.

EXTENDING ONESELF

Watch an animal stretch itself. Cats are notorious stretchers. Note how they arch their backs, then stretch them out. Flexibility is important to most mammals. Stretching gently on a daily basis increases our range of motion. *Ask the Doctor at:* www.health.harvard.edu states that stretching before a muscle is warmed up can injure it. If you exercise and *then* stretch, your muscles are warmed up with blood flow and the tissues are more pliable.

Never bounce while stretching. Instead, hold the stretch for 30 seconds. Don't stretch past where it is comfortable; pain does not lead to gain; it leads to further pain and chronic injuries. Find a physical therapist who can help you work out a plan for your particular age and condition. It is a great investment in your future.

THE COLORS OF HUMANITY

If you ask ten people to mix "skin color" paint, you will probably arrive at ten different hues. Yet at some time, most of us try to draw or paint humans. Crayons labeled "skin color" are woefully inadequate, regardless of whether your skin tends to be pale or dark. The following is a great exercise for adults and kids (age six and up).

Learn to mix skin colors. You will need:

1. Several jars (or tubes, depending upon your medium) of paint in the following colors: White, Cadmium Yellow, Cadmium Red Medium, Ultramarine Blue, Yellow Ochre and Burnt Sienna.

2. A brush appropriate for your medium.

3. A palette on which you will mix your paint.

4. Craft sticks for mixing.

Your first task is to mix the color of your skin, noting what colors you used and in what proportion. Next, find good color photos of people with skin colors different from yours and try mixing those. Better still, do this with a group of people with varying skin colors.

Note your findings and compare each person's skin color you have mixed. Unless you are a Fauve painter, like Gaugin, you will be using the same pigments for all the skin colors you mix, but in varying amounts. Ask the kids if they can draw any conclusions from this.

A JOYFUL MOMENT IN TIME

Find some joy in your life this weekend. Then tell yourself, "Right now, I am truly happy." This doesn't mean that your whole life is terrific; it means that for several minutes or longer, you are feeling good. Most of us have moments like this during our day which we never notice.

Paying attention to happiness causes our brains to communicate to our bodies that we are happy, releasing a flood of endorphins. In other words, telling yourself when things are good actually makes you feel better overall.

THE LEADER OF THE PACK

Look up the word, "demagogue." Locate the Greek origins of the word. Make a list of characteristics antithetical to a demagogue. Scan various news sources over the past year for contemporary leaders with these characteristics.

Next, study the histories of countries that were led by demagogues. Learn as much as possible about the fate of those countries. Start a conversation with your friends about American history and whether there are people in our government who seek to become demagogues.

Understanding and coming to terms with America's would-be-leaders is necessary for our democracy to function as intended. Becoming involved in protecting that democracy makes us active participants in our own future.

OF ETHICS AND MORALITY

Let's examine the word, "Integrity." Read So-Young Kang's short article in her 2016 Huffpost blog, "The True Meaning of Integrity." Spend some time this evening reviewing your day. Ask yourself, "Have I behaved with integrity throughout the day? What examples are there of others who did or did not?"

How many times have you asked yourself or another person what they think of a certain individual and their reply was, "I guess he's/she's ok." This non-answer shows the intellectual sloppiness of Americans who have blurred the line between what is and is not acceptable in our leaders, our celebrities, and ourselves. We lose the ability to trust when we are let down repeatedly by people lacking integrity.

Write the names of ten individuals you know personally or read about frequently in the news whom you admire. Spend some time this month noting specific incidents in which these people have behaved with integrity. Describe what they did, when they did it, and why they acted this way. What would happen if we demanded integrity from our politicians, our religious and business leaders?

What if we, ourselves, from this day forward, made a solemn pledge to be an example of integrity for others? What if we stopped saying, "That's just the way things are these days?"

THE REAL ESTATE OF THE SELF

The next time you are in the company of others, take note of how much space you occupy. What things do you carry with you? (Briefcases, backpacks, pocketbooks, strollers, shopping bags, pets…etc.). How far is your noise traveling? Are you talking on a cell phone, listening to music, speaking with others, children, or pets? Do you have an odor, such as fragrance, strong food smells; are you sweaty from exercise…etc.?

Consider how much you overlap into other people's space.

LITTER PICKIN 'PARTY

Recruit a team of children (having obtained parental permissions). Find two or three adult friends who can help. Have everyone pack a picnic lunch and a beverage. Buy a supply of strong garbage bags, rubber gloves, and some hand wipes. Choose a location that is safe but where people litter, such as a public park, an empty lot or the woods.

Now have each team choose a captain. Each captain will confer with their adult group leader as to where they should go. The captain will be in charge of keeping the time. The groups should spread out away from each other. At the signal, each group will go about picking up litter. The rules: nothing sharp or with food on it; only dry refuse should go in the bags. At the time decided upon, all teams should meet at a designated area. Then gloves get discarded in a bag, hands get cleaned and disinfected and everyone has lunch. Bring along plenty of pencils and paper.

After lunch, ask the kids to record their impressions of the day, so far. What were their thoughts as they picked up the trash? Did they picture the individual who threw the stuff out? Why do they think people do that kind of thing, and what should we do to persuade people to stop doing it? Then, go home and lay the trash outside where you can have a good look at it. Give each person a large piece of cardboard and some duct tape or fast-drying glue. Using a fresh pair of gloves, each person may make a picture or a collage using thrown-away litter. Ask your local school to post the art with a big banner reading: "Don't litter!"

INTERPERSONAL DIFFICULTIES

If you have a situation in which you are having problems with another individual and you have tried to find a solution on your own, but have failed, get help from others. Find a professional with whom you can talk. The problem might be caused by you, or it might be the other person. The main thing is to get some objective insight or perspective.

If the person with whom you have the problem refuses to talk it out or work on making things better, you must decide how much time and energy you will expend on them. Once you have exhausted your time limit, move on.

Sometimes you just have to agree to disagree, but your life should be spent around people who make you happy and vice versa.

WILD BEAUTY

Make a wildflower bouquet for someone. Pick your wildflowers carefully. In other words, do your homework to make sure you aren't picking something rare or important to the survival of a species. Do pick from areas where the wildflowers are not wanted, like abandoned lots or pastures or fields people don't frequent.

Never pick ALL the blooms of a plant. Pick grasses and weeds and interesting branches to fill out the bouquet. Goldenrod, Queen Anne's Lace, Indian Paintbrush, and grains like Oats and Barley add texture and color. If you find a field of Daisies or Black-Eyed Susans, you can add these too.

Make sure no one receiving the bouquet has allergies to any of the plants. Cattail makes a nice accent. Whatever you can find that grows abundantly wild in your area makes the best wildflower bouquets. Give the bouquet to someone who needs it to remind them of the world outside.

YOUR PIECE OF SKY

Buy a really colorful umbrella. Those sold in the gift shops of museums or from their online stores, and at high-end grocers like Whole Foods can be a little pricey, but you can hunt through chain stores and department stores. Umbrellas are also to be found at consignment shops and second-hand stores.

Golf umbrellas, the large ones, can be purchased in some grocery chains. It doesn't matter where you buy your umbrella; the point is to buy something that reminds you of being a child at a circus and having someone hand you a big, shiny, colorful balloon.

Think of your umbrella as this balloon, so that every time you go outside in the driving rain or in a gentle mist, you will think of how you felt holding onto the string of your own colorful piece of the sky that dances with the wind.

CHEER

Be supportive of people around you who are trying to make a change in their lives. If they are trying to eat healthier, drink less alcohol, use fewer recreational drugs, exercise more, or get more sleep, do not tempt, tease or discourage them.

Encourage their small successes and let them know you are proud of them. Once the person feels as if they are achieving their goal, celebrate with them!

LET THEM EAT BREAD

Google a simple yeast bread recipe; something that rises once. Make a list of all the ingredients you will need and assemble all your tools: bowls, wooden spoons, measuring cups, etc. This will be a hand-made bread, even if you have a dough mixer. Give yourself several hours to make your bread. Read through the recipe first to get down the order of the steps.

Make sure the temperature of the water for dissolving the yeast is correct. You may use a bread thermometer. You will require a working surface. A breadboard or a marble-top counter that is very clean will do. Once you have combined and mixed all your ingredients and the dough has risen, punch it down and on your floured surface, you will knead the dough.

Ideally, you want something table-height to knead your bread on, so that your back doesn't get sore. Now, after flouring the kneading surface, pour out the dough onto the floured surface, piling some extra flour alongside. Keep your hands as non-sticky as possible by flouring them. If the dough begins to stick to them, flour the ball of dough lightly. Wash, dry, and re-flour your hands.

Gather the dough, hands cupped over top, and sink the heels of your hands into the dough, pushing down and forward. The dough will bulge up under the fingers, which you will use to pull the bulge towards you over the place you pushed down. Round up the dough and repeat the pushing down, pulling towards you, and rounding up. Keep dusting the breadboard with flour so the bread doesn't stick.

Enjoy the feel of the dough, which is a living thing. Note the texture as you knead, feeling it change from lumpy to smooth. Pay attention to the interaction of your body with the dough. Keep kneading for 5-10 minutes until the dough feels alive and silky. Follow your recipe, either letting the dough rest or forming it into a loaf, or placing it into a greased, floured pan before cooking it. The point is to enjoy the connection with a food which all the world's peoples have made for eons.

Once you have mastered making a simple loaf, teach someone else to do it who needs to feel as if they have accomplished something.

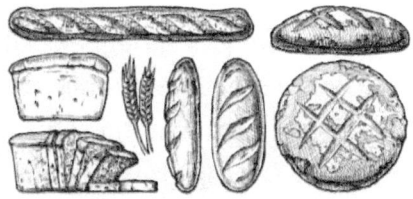

ROAD RAGE

Summer brings out the kid in all of us; especially when we're driving our cars. However, when one is behind the wheel of a vehicle, one must drive like an adult. This means taking a deep breath during the endless traffic jams and not getting even with other drivers who cut us off or drive slowly in the left lane, refusing to yield to faster drivers.

It also means if you are a pokey driver, be aware of drivers around you and let them pass. If you are a biker, resist the temptation to show off, peeling out when the light turns green or driving in-between stopped cars in traffic slow downs.

If you are following a motorcycle and you are in a 4-wheel vehicle, you need to stay far enough back that you could avoid hitting the biker if he/she fell over. Think of yourself as protecting the motorcycle driver ahead of you; they are vulnerable out there amongst all the cars and trucks.

Should you encounter an erratic or thoughtless driver, try to write down or record their license plate and note where you are. Pull over and call 911. You aren't not "ratting someone out;" your call could save lives. Someone acting irresponsibly on the road puts all of us in danger. Getting a ticket or a warning might prevent a tragedy later. A repeat offender might get removed from the road. Help preserve lives this summer.

A HELPFUL PHRASE

Practice saying the phrase, "This too shall pass." When you find yourself feeling helpless, as in when you are stuck taking a boring but required class, workshop, or conference, remember this phrase. When you are in pain, have suffered a loss, when you must put up with a colicky infant, an irritating relative or a partner who likes to relate the entire plot of a movie they just watched, say this silently to yourself. It will get you through a lot of trying times.

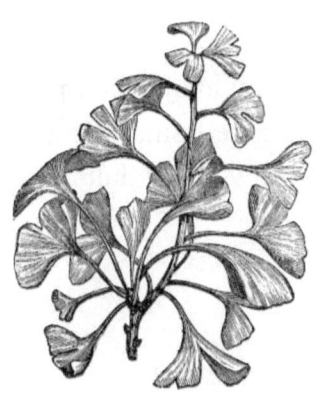

IT'S A BIG COUNTRY!

If you frequent family-style restaurants with your kids or grand-kids, bring along a drawing pad and several crayons. When the food has been eaten, take out the drawing pad and say loudly enough for people around your table and their kids to hear "Who can draw a map of the United States?"

If the kids at other tables look interested, check with their parents to see if it's ok for them to join in the fun. Turn the pad horizontally and place four dots where, roughly, the coasts, the Canadian border, and the bottom of Texas will be. Give one child a crayon and have them first draw a rough outline of America. Ask if they can draw their state. Then have a few parents to do the same thing. Give everyone positive feedback, even if they think California is on the East coast.

Find something nice to say about each person's map. Give each person their drawing to take home. Most likely, one of the kids will locate a map and show their adults where everything is supposed to be.

UN-PLANNED OBSOLESCENCE

Look at the front legs of several dogs. See if they have a claw several inches above the paw on the inside of the leg. This is called a dew claw and is often removed because these extra claws can get caught on things later in life and are not usually functional.

We humans, too, have what I think of as dew claws; behaviors which, throughout our evolution, may have been useful once but are not now, and may even cause us harm. "Might makes right" is one of the worst of the dew claws of humanity. This accounts for the oppression of women, children, the or the elderly.

Like dogs, we have evolved to the point where a holdover from the past is causing us harm. Make a list of at least five of your own dew claws. Next to each, write, in a simple statement, why you have this behavior. Next, write why the behavior is undesirable. Finally, make a plan to eliminate each dew claw.

THE PROXIMITY PRINCIPLE

Hold onto the people you love. Do not lose touch with old friends or family. Electronic devices are wonderful for people communicating with loved ones far away, however, there is no substitute for face-to-face contact. Humans communicate not only through words; body language and the un-amplified timbre of an individual's voice carry a world of meaning. Maintaining a true bond and deep understanding requires showing up.

With loneliness on the rise and the traditional structures that used to bring people together waning, religious institutions, clubs and even public schooling being less popular or carried on through a computer, the personal contact necessary for Homo Sapiens and other social animal species to develop empathy, clear communication and deep bonds is often lacking. Spend some time listing people with whom you haven't communicated in a long time. Choose to contact them, although it may feel awkward. You have nothing to lose, and you could re-establish an important relationship. If you value someone, don't lose touch, literally. Life is fragile, precious, and short.

ARRETON CHURCH, ISLE OF WIGHT.

A SMALL WORLD

On the next sunny day, go outside with a small plastic bag and a big spoon or a trowel. Find a place where it is legal for you to dig a hole in the ground. Make sure the earth you are digging is the native earth of your area. If you are in a city, find a construction area, or an abandoned lot. Dig up about a cup of the soil. Now, look around for a small native plant. This could be a weed or a cactus or moss or a small wildflower. (Note: only take something that grows in profusion, as some wildflowers are endangered).

Buy a glass fishbowl and put some small marbles or pebbles in the bottom for drainage. Add your dirt and whatever plant you brought home. Water the soil, being careful not to overdo it. Cover the top with a piece of plastic and put the bowl near a source of sunlight comparable to where you dug the plant and dirt. Keep watch over the little world you made, removing the plastic if it looks too wet and adding water if it is too dry. Spend some time at eye level with your little world. How does it look close up? How does it smell? Picture yourself as a tiny creature inhabiting that world, dependent upon the correct amount of oxygen, water, and edible plant protein. Consider the ways in which this applies to our own world.

CORE DATA

Let us consider the kiwi (the fruit, not the bird). From the genus Actinidia, the fruit originated in China and can be cultivated in temperate climates. About the size of a chicken egg, kiwis have brown or gold-ish skin and can be slightly fuzzy or smooth. When you cut them open, they are green or golden-green inside with a lighter core and a circle of black or red edible seeds. The texture and flavor are something like that of a green grape.

Kiwis are delicious fruits, but here's the problem: they are sold when they are still too hard to eat. Each week, buy a kiwi. Develop a sense of touch in order to know when is the right time to eat them. Squeeze them gently. If they feel rock-hard, wait a day or more, leaving them un-refrigerated. When they feel slightly soft, cut one open. Sometimes the fruit will be ripe, but the core is still too hard; a problem that can defy eating without making a mess. If you wait too long, the kiwi will slice easily but will taste slightly spoiled and mealy. Knowing when to slice a kiwi takes a great deal of practice.

A great kiwi, ripened to perfection makes it all worth it. It takes experience with kiwis to learn the skill of knowing when to eat them. Like all things in life, knowledge follows from experience. Those who claim they can do things better because they *lack* experience, as well as the people who believe them just end up with a lot of sour, rotten fruit.

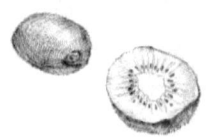

UNCHAINED MELODY

Learn a comforting song; something that sustains people during hard times. When the 9/11 attacks occurred, professional balladeer Linda Russell led people on the Upper West Side of New York, in singing, "Amazing Grace" as they walked down Broadway together, watching the sky over lower Manhattan blacken with smoke. Music, even at the darkest of times, has the power to strengthen us. Spirituals sustained enslaved people through some of the toughest times one can imagine. The Blues, Hip-hop and rap have afforded generations expression of their everyday experience.

Once I attended the funeral of a friend who died suddenly. It was raining. We who attended the burial were in shock as we walked into the tiny graveyard surrounded by woods. Then, our attention was drawn to a Dixieland band that accompanied the hearse down the lane. We may not have known the words, but we understood how our friend would have loved that music, which spoke of the universality of life and death, and of how we must go on, despite the most painful of sorrows. Learn a song. Music is a lifeline we can toss to each other.

THE LAST DROP

Fill a glass with water to the top. Using a small spoon, being careful not to make the glass overflow, add more water, drop by drop until the top surface of the water begins to bulge upward in the center. This surface "skin" is called the meniscus and is caused by the surface tension of water. See how far you can go before your meniscus breaks and the water spills over the rim.

Now imagine yourself as the glass and the water as stressors. Recall a situation in which you handled the stress until finally your own emotional skin was stretched to the point of rupturing. List five major stressors in your life, for example, being trapped in a loud environment, feeling rushed, pain, etc. Gauge your limit in each type of stressful situation.

Choose one of your most common stressors and take note of every time that stress occurs during the day. How many incidents were you able to handle before your own surface tension was broken and you cried, lost your temper, got drunk, or took it out on others? Keep a little chart and figure out just how far you can go with each of your worst stressors. Do not allow yourself to reach that line.

A KNOTTY PROBLEM

Teach a child to tie their shoelaces.

1. Place a child's and one of your own untied shoes next to each other on a table that is a comfortable height for the child. With the child next to you, ask them to copy what you do.

2. Take the right lace in your right hand and the left in your left hand. If they can do this, say, "Good!"

3. Cross your right lace over the left, in an X. Then, pull it under the left lace towards your tummy. Pull gently on each shoelace, making a simple knot. If the child is left-handed, cross the left lace over the right and tuck it under the right. NOTE: Do not go past what a child can do comfortably. If this is as far as they can get, say, "Oh boy! You can tie your shoes halfway!" Do something else, returning to this skill until it is comfortable for the child. Once that is the case and the child has tied a simple knot with the shoelaces, proceed to step number 4 and go on from there.

4. Put both laces down and pick up either the shoelace now on the right or the left, (right for right-handers; left for left-handers). Holding both hands, fold the lace in your right hand against itself about an inch from the knot, making a loop, which you will pinch in-between your right-hand thumb and forefinger.

5. Pull the shoelace that is in your left hand towards you and slide it over the right thumbnail, wrapping it three-quarters of the way around the pinched loop. With your left index finger, poke that lace under itself along the side of your thumb towards your tummy. This will form the second loop. Let go of it and grab the top of the first loop with your left hand. Let go of the first loop with your right hand and grasp the second loop.

6. With each hand holding a loop, pull them tight. For left-handed people, reverse the hands in steps number 4 and number 5. Tying one's own shoes is extremely satisfying for a child to learn, creating more independence in dressing. Eye-hand coordination develops at different ages, so go slowly and be extremely patient in teaching.

REPLENISH

When you are exhausted, as all of us are from time to time, find someone to fill in for you so you can have a break. You may trade with them; "You take the kids somewhere on Tuesday and I'll take them somewhere on Friday."

Request a personal or vacation day for self-renewal. Think of yourself as a pitcher of water; the water of life, from which others need to drink. If the pitcher isn't refilled, all will suffer from thirst.

Ask for help when you need time off and then help others when they, too, must rest.

IN SICKNESS

Be strong during health crises. Reach out to family and friends. If you are the person going through a crisis, pay close attention to little things, like the smell of food or the feel of your bed. Read a long story, or better yet, a series of engaging books. Watch movies. The idea is to set short goals for yourself, such as, "I will spend an hour reading. Then I will make myself a cup of tea." These little goals give you purpose and move the day along. If someone you know is going through a health problem, let them know they can call you, and be sure to check in on them. Life is very hard at times. We are all part of the human family and need to support each other.

TRUE LEADERSHIP

List effective leaders in our government and your own personal life. Identify what makes them good. Dog obedience books talk about strong leadership being necessary for training intelligent creatures. The books list qualities of good and bad leadership; identical to characteristics needed to be a teacher or leader of humans. Bad trainers/teachers/leaders are often weak and insecure, making idle threats, or blaming the dogs or their human charges for bad behavior. This would-be leader may have knowledge but cannot command respect. Equally poor is the bully, who imposes authority by shouting and punishing. This kind of leader causes dogs to bite and people to back-bite. Good leaders are secure in themselves and clear about their goals and expectations. They establish consequences for negative behavior, but their emphasis is on positive reinforcement.

Master canine trainer, Celeste Meade-Maurer, states that, "To allow the behavior is to train the behavior." Good leaders do their homework before teaching and, while they continue learning on the job, are not trying to train themselves on the job. They are firm but patient, paying attention to an individual's problems. Good trainers and leaders demand respect for themselves and teach respect for others. In your notebook, make a list of leaders in your world. Which category do they fall into? Find examples from your own life, from literature, or real events in the news.

Next, write a little blurb about why you feel these people fit into each category. If you are in a position of leadership, which type are you? Who are the people or groups the leaders on your list have impacted? Finally, draw some conclusions regarding their effect upon the world.

BEING A BUFFER

If you know or work with anyone who has a sick family member, especially a child, cut them some slack. Be kind to them. Ask if there is something you can do to help, such as shopping, or taking them to a doctor if they need a ride.

Try to take pressure off them for the time being. Once their loved one is well, they will be productive again. You can be their hero.

AN ADVENTURE FROM HOME

Choose a historical time that intrigues you. Do a little research at your on-line library to find a really interesting book about the period or, if your book is historical fiction, about a character, well-known or not. Be sure the author is an engaging writer who is excited about the topic and has portrayed the period accurately.

Set aside a period each day where you can sit somewhere quietly and indulge in the pleasure of a good read. Explore the food, dress, and culture of your chosen period. Now, get your family involved. Ask each person to pick a country and a period to explore. Take a field trip to a museum or an art gallery. You may take this exercise as far as you like, exploring the music, food and clothing of the period. Everyone might make a costume from old clothes. The more you invest in doing this, the more your world expands.

STAY HYDRATED

Drink one more glass of water today than you usually do. A human body is roughly sixty percent water. We are *of* the water and require it for our innards to function properly. Being on the run as much as we are, we don't drink enough to keep ourselves healthy.

Find a drinking buddy in your home or office. Make a pact that you will meet for a drink of water at a specific time each day.

SEVERE WEATHER FRIENDS

Collect acorns that are unblemished. Make sure there are no tiny holes in them. You could involve your family in an acorn hunt come autumn, especially the kids. Wash and dry the acorns and place them in freezer bags in your freezer. When it snows or freezes this winter, scatter defrosted acorns where there are trees for little critters. Do this far away from your house so as not to invite rodents to come in for a visit!

Should we have a severe winter with a great deal of snow you can also make the following recipe for wild birds and spread it on the bark or branches of trees: a block of suet and a cup of fresh-ground, unsalted peanuts mixed in a bowl by hand. Toss in a handful of cranberries, sesame seeds, or sunflower seeds. Enjoy the variety of birds that come to feast.

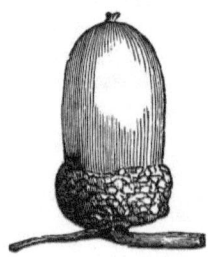

I, ME, MINE!

Using a watch with a timer, record in a small notebook how many times you use the personal pronoun "I" in a 15-minute conversation with someone. Next, set the timer for 10 minutes, then 5 minutes, doing the same thing. If you notice that you dominate the conversation with first- person references, you might want to ask a family member or close friend to assist you in breaking this habit. Ask them to check the amount of time you spend listening rather than speaking when you are chatting with them.

This works best if you do it over the course of a week, so that you will forget you are being monitored. Once you have some knowledge of how much you share conversations, as opposed to dominating them, you can teach yourself to listen more often.

AS GOOD AS YOUR WORD

Make a list of your commitments. As you fulfill each, check it off the list. When you promise to do something, follow through. Many of us make vows we have little intention of fulfilling. Think before you give your word.

Before making a commitment to a child, another human, or an animal, consider its ramifications. Counting on each other's word is essential for civil society. Knowing that you keep your word will engender self-respect.

OUR GANG

Suggest to your class, office, religious sports team or social group that you compile a scrapbook together with photos of your members. Ask each person to write an abbreviated autobiography that includes what their best experience was within the group, who their friends are and why, and something positive they have learned since joining.

Add to the scrapbook over the years, having people bring in family photos, pictures of pets, and lists of their favorite foods. These days, people spending time in each other's presence are like horses in their separate stalls: in unconnected proximity.

Our epidemic of loneliness needs to be addressed and cured. We can start by getting to know the people with whom we work and play: our "gang."

HOMEMAKERS

If you buy a stove or refrigerator, keep the cardboard box. Gather together some sharp scissors and a mat knife, a magic marker, a roll of duct tape (you can buy it in various colors now) a roll of packaging tape, and a pad of colored construction paper all the same color.

Now you need two or three kids, from six to eight years old (yours or neighborhood kids). Get permission from their parents first. Explain you are building a cardboard house. If the parents agree, tell the kids you need some help to build a house. If they regard you with disgust and go back to their digital devices, start without them. Either work outside on your property where the kids can watch or indoors near the kids.

1. Place the box in front of you and determine where your door should be.

2. Draw the door with your marker, remembering that you can have Dutch doors, round doors like Hobbits, or whatever you like.

3. Cut the door out with your mat knife, remembering to leave one side attached, so it can close. (Important note: You will do ALL the cutting, keeping hold of the scissors or knife).

4. Cut a doorknob hole. By now, you will have workers, or, at least, an audience.

5. Ask where the windows should go. Get some help drawing them. Then cut them out. Save the pieces, which you will cut in half vertically for window shutters.

6. For the roof, open the top of the box and tape the two long together, outside and in with duct tape to make a peak.

7. Fold up the two short box sides. With your marker, trace the roof lines and cut off the extra cardboard, leaving two triangles. Tape these to the roof pieces, inside and out.

8. Use the construction paper to cut shingles and, starting with the lowest row, tape them to the roof in lines, overlapping the taped part.

Your crew must decide upon other features, a chimney, fence, window boxes, painting the house, etc. The kids will learn to exercise their creativity, decision-making and hone their artistic vision and imaginations. You will learn how much fun you can have using inexpensive materials.

AND THAT IS WHY I SAY

Remember when you were very young. Think of the title of one of the books that made an impression upon you. If you don't have a copy, look for the book in your library, or online. Re-read the book. When you are done, ask yourself what the author's point was. You can determine this by finishing the statement as if you were the author: "And that is why I say _____."

Sometimes, the answer will be the moral of the story. Sometimes the author wants to instruct or create in you a certain emotion. Now, apply the story to everyday life. Feel free to modernize it with real characters from the news or from your family.

INTRUSIVE INDIVIDUALS

Consider the word, "nosey." List five people in your life whom you consider to be nosey. Write a sentence or two explaining what makes them seem nosey. Then add how this makes you feel about them. How do you react towards them? Are you angry, amused, offended, or put in a difficult position because of their nosiness?

People who either are unaware of your boundaries or do not respect them can make you irritable and anxious. Become your own advocate. Plan several ways of dealing with these folk's behavior before it re-occurs. Finally, list five occasions in which *you* have been the nosey individual. What were the results?

STRONG VALUES

Consider the word, "value." We use it as a verb, an adjective, and a noun: "I *value* your friendship," "We use *value* brands, instead of premium, to save money," and, "Do you have anything of *value* in your purse?" Originating from the Latin word, "valere," it translates as, "be whole, be strong."

We use it today in math, as in assigning a value, and in art, where value relates to the lightness or darkness of a hue. In your notebook, make a list of ten things you value. These can be ideas, people, or material things. Do the same exercise using "value" as an adjective, then as a noun.

Read what you have written. Imagine that someone else made this list. Would you guess this person to be strong and whole? If not, what steps should they take to become more complete?

INFLAMMATORY FABRICATIONS

Let us consider the verb, "lie." *Merriam-Webster* defines it as "making an untrue statement with the intention to deceive," or "creating a false or misleading impression." The word is of uncertain origin, not found in Latin, Greek, or Sanskrit. The *Online Etymology Dictionary* lists it as: "late 12th c. Old English *ligan,* earlier *leogan,* "deceive, belie, betray."

Everyone reading this has told a lie at some time. Prior to the internet and social media, our news sources were restricted to gossip, television, radio, and newspapers. If a blatant lie was told, it came to the attention of people readily. Certain news sources were viewed by most as trustworthy, whether or not one agreed with the news they delivered. However, lies have become easier to spread, since ferreting out truth can be time-consuming.

Take out your notebook and spend a week, a month or more recording lies you read or hear in the media or online. For each lie you record, you must prove that it is a purposefully told untruth. Make three columns in your book. In column number 1, list the lie, where you heard or read it, and from whom. In column number 2, write a few sentences explaining what this person (or group) had to gain from the lie. In column number 3, examine the possible effect this lie could have on you and your community. As lying in public has become commonplace, ask yourself if you or people you know have developed this bad habit. When you hear yourself telling an untruth, stop and say, "Wait; that's not exactly right. I misspoke." Others will begin trusting your word.

THEIR OWN SPECIAL THING

In your travels, take note of someone whom you think does not often get praised. This might be the near stranger you see every day at work or school, or it could be someone in your family. We often assume family members can read our minds; they know automatically that we love and appreciate them. Unfortunately, one often hears bereaved relatives say, "If only I had told them how much they meant to me."

Observe their manner, their voice, their neatness, their attitude, and their efficiency. Identify one special thing about them. Give them a sincere compliment, looking them in the eyes.

DOWN CAME A SPIDER

Get a group of kids you know together and form a spider club. Remember those parental permissions come first! Go on a photo hunt for spiders, particularly the ones that spin webs out of silk. You may use your cell phone or a camera. Some good times to find them are just after a rainstorm, a frost, a sunrise or at dusk. If you don't have access to the outdoors, a cellar or an attic makes for good hunting.

Once you find your subject, do not touch the web or disturb its maker. The idea is to get some great shots of these critters which you can enlarge and study. Spiders use their webs to capture unsuspecting prey. They can spin six different types of silk. Spider silk is five times stronger than steel weighing the same amount. Many of us fear spiders although spiders don't attack humans unless threatened. Spiders have a bad rap, despite the fact that they eat disease-spreading insects and bugs that destroy crops. Have each club member adopt a type of spider and look up all they can find about them. Locate an entomologist by calling a college or an agricultural agency near you. Invite them to present a talk.

Too many of us fear our eight-legged friends; the best way to conquer fear of the unknown is to get to know and understand them.

FEATHERED WONDERS

Collect several big, colorful, interesting feathers. If you can't find any outside, craft and party stores sell them. Pack two or three in a plastic lunch bag to carry with you. At some point, you will cross paths with a small child who could use a feather. Ask their parents first if they may have yours.

A crying child will often stop fussing, especially if you "fly" the feather in front of them. A non-crying child will look at you in wonder and accept the feather as though it were a sudden miraculous gift.

ONE SMALL LIFE

Choose a plant native to your area and immerse yourself in learning about it. This could be a rare wildflower, a prevalent weed, something that is invasive (not really native but that's ok) or something that previously existed before Europeans came along and eliminated it.

Get a notebook. On one page, do a drawing or paste a picture of your subject. On another page, write all you can find about its origins; what family it comes from and what its relatives are. Does this plant exist in other places? Was it purposely cultivated and improved, like maize? On another page, record all its uses to the planet. What is its role? Who feeds upon, shelters in, or builds with it? Consider what would happen if it suddenly disappeared. How would this change the earth? If your plant was introduced from another place, who did it and when? Why? What is the effect upon your area now? How has this plant adapted to human life?

Once we focus on a living thing, it stops being "just another weed" and we realize that it has its own unique role in our environment, as do we.

UNBURIED TREASURE

Collect dimes in a jar. From time to time, "plant" ten of them where a stranger will find them.

If you can watch from a distance, take pleasure in how happy people are when they come upon an unexpected treasure, however small. A wondrous discovery can color a person's whole day.

LEASHES

Let us consider leashes. Dogs are required to be on a leash in most public places. From the dog's point of view, running wild, not coming when called, jumping on people, and chewing up inedible objects are fun things to do. However, in doing so, they could get hit by cars, run off and become lost, frighten a non-dog lover, knock someone down, or end up in the doggie hospital.

We humans establish mores for ourselves. These function as leashes, since people don't always understand or accept the rules that have been decided upon by their culture for things to run smoothly. Children often rail against learning manners. "Why, *why* must I use a fork instead of my fingers? Why can't I get up while others are eating and run around the table? Why can't I yell when and where I feel like it?"

Most of us have chafed against rules we feel limit our personal freedoms. Adults may question why they can't play music in their apartments so loudly that it bothers their neighbors. Some people feel they have every right to speak on their cell phones in areas where others are forced to listen. "Why," they demand to know, "is it anybody's business what I do with my life?" The answer is that our lives are better because of those manners, mores and rules. Civility towards others lubricates a society, making it run smoothly. Americans have the right to question authority and change laws that do more bad than good. Make a list of the leashes you wear at different times. Which of them do you consider to be necessary? Which would you most like to eliminate? Now consider what would happen if there were no mores for you, for your community, your state, or your country. Imagine how each would be impacted.

BELOVED STRANGER

The next time you are in your car, pretend the car driving in front of you holds someone about whom you care a great deal. As the person following them, you can, through lack of consideration or impatience, startle or distract them, causing them to have an accident. Don't tailgate, or honk, even if they are driving below the speed limit. There may be a reason for their caution. Drive as if their life depends on it.

LEARN THROUGH WATCHING

Go to a public place, like a park, a playground, or anywhere you may observe people. Find five examples of people being frustrated with someone or something. This usually involves impatience with others, such as children, dogs, slow walkers, drivers or having to wait on a line. In each instance, describe the people involved as best you can. What is the conflict between them? How does this play out? Then, go somewhere you can contemplate what you have observed.

Write a small paragraph in which you imagine how things could have gone more smoothly between your characters. What could they have said or done differently? Finally, carry your notepad around for a week and find five examples of situations in which *you* became impatient. How did you react? Did this result in making things better? If not, what have you learned that you can do the next time you find yourself in similar situations?

NOT SO HOT

If you are suffering from the heat this summer (since data confirms that the earth has grown hotter every summer now for nearly a decade), get a group of people together to buy t-shirts that will fit each member. In a craft store, buy fabric lettering paint. Assemble some tables, buckets of water, sponges, and soap for clean-up.

Have each member of your group pick an animal and a phrase expressing something about the climate that relates to that animal. For example, you could draw a horse of a mule or a donkey and under it write: "Too hot to trot? Reverse climate change!" If no one can draw, find a photo of the animal and trace the outline. You can paint its silhouette, which can be very effective. You could write, "the Dog Days of June, July, Aug. & Sept? Fight climate change!" or paint tropical birds, such as parrots and write, "This Ain't the Tropics; 'Just *Feels* Like it! Reverse Climate Change." If you live on a coast, you can do the same thing with images relating to rising sea levels. You could draw fish and write "Fish Gotta Swim... Can You? ... Fight climate change!"

You get the idea: be creative and proclaim the message. Who knows? Your design might end up becoming a famous image! Use the same idea for flags, banners, posters, or greeting cards.

IN MEMORIAM

Find out what past events occurred in your city or town. If someone lived or died in a certain place, or an important historical event occurred there, you might consider making a cairn as a marker. The word "cairn" comes from the Scottish word, carn, or heap. Cairns are small piles of stones in the shape of a horn, as they become smaller on top like the tip of a horn.

Your cairn does not have to be large. Of course, cairns are transitory in a place like a city and should only be made in a safe, out-of-the-way area, like a park or a vacant lot. People will come along and knock it down eventually. But while you are building it, someone may question you, enabling you to share a little history of the person or event you are memorializing. Think of it as a tribute or, if you prefer, a prayer for the persons you are remembering.

A RHYMING GAME

Buy a box of pencils and sharpen them. Buy an inexpensive pad of white paper. Take both with you when you ride on public transportation. When you are stuck on a subway, in traffic on a bus or have a long ride by train, look around for a child who looks bored. Ask the adult with them for permission to have their child make a list of words that rhyme. If they agree, have the child think of a one-syllable name of an animal and hand them a pencil and a piece of paper, if they're old enough to write.

For example, they might say, "cow." Then you say, "now." Then it's their turn. Ask for 10 one-syllable words. Then go to 2-syllable words or phrases that rhyme, like, "eyebrow!" or "bow-wow." List as many as possible, then go on to 3 syllables. Ask the young person to pick another one-syllable word of their choice and do the same thing.

When you have several pages filled with rhymes, give them a pencil and a blank piece of paper and ask them to use the words to write a poem or a rap. Suggest they try it on their own or with friends at home.

FRAME OF REFERENCE

If one asks a 1st grader to draw a table that is before them, they will often draw a square with lines representing legs sticking outwards. They are not drawing what they *see*; they are drawing what they *know*. This, depending upon one's culture, appears wrong (unless one is a Cubist) because we are used to the Western world's system of perspective, attributed to 15th c. artist, Filippo Brunelleschi. He traced the lines of reflected buildings on his mirror, demonstrating that they appear to recede towards one single point (which he called the vanishing point) on the horizon.

We have adopted this view as reality. In other cultures, one may depict several viewpoints at once. Each culture considers their system of depicting the world as the correct one. Take a piece of paper and find a three-dimensional object such as a shoebox to use as a model. Place it on a table or a shelf parallel to the shelf's edge. Stand or sit so that your model is directly in front of you. Using a crayon, marker or pencil, draw what you see. Now move several feet to either side and again, draw your model. You are seeing it from your perspective. Now, on a different sheet of paper, draw not what you see from where you are positioned, but what you *know* about the box. You should end up with two extremely different drawings of the same object.

In other words, both are attempts at depicting reality, but go about it differently. Ask yourself, "Is one drawing more true than the other?" Consider how everyone interprets reality depending upon their perspective.

GIFT-WRAPPED

Cut off your hair. This is for those of you with long, strong hair. Lara, a lovely woman with gorgeous rich brown hair, grows it out and then every few years, has it cut and donates it to be made into wigs for those who have had chemo.

Imagine how great you would feel being enveloped in someone's beautiful hair while you were growing your own back or receiving treatment, as though the spirit of the generous donor was wrapped around you, like a protective embrace, encouraging your body to recover. For the donor, the benefit speaks for itself.

OUR BODY SENSE

Consider how tender the human body is. A paper cut hurts really badly. Toothaches incapacitate us. Luckily, once we are pain-free, our bodies immediately forget the pain and go on as though it never occurred.

If you are without pain at this time, consider the other sensations your body is experiencing right now. Appreciate the feel of water on your skin. Enjoy the sun's warmth on your face. Inhale the air and feel it tickle your nostrils. Now stretch yourself, the way a cat does: purposefully, luxuriously, one part at a time. Yawn and notice how good your throat feels when you don't have a cold. Rub your feet, pulling on each toe. Stretch out your fingers to their fullest extent, then make a fist. Take a deep breath and feel your lungs expanding. Rub your fingers through your hair, slowly massaging your scalp.

Lastly, lie down and listen to the beating of your own heart. It is a miracle, isn't it? Cherish the way you feel when you are healthy and use that memory when you are unwell, looking forward to your health returning.

THE NAME GAME

Make a book of names. If you have difficulty recalling people's names, carry a small notebook and pencil with you (or cell-phone) to record the names of those you meet. Write a little description of them (never anything that would hurt feelings if found!) to help prompt your memory.

No one is offended when you ask, "Do you mind if I write down your name so I will be sure to recall it?" Most people are pleased that you wish to remember them. This is especially helpful when people we meet have unfamiliar names. Knowing another person's name whom you have met before gives you confidence.

THANKS

Remember to say, "Thank you." The way you say it is important. Look the person in the eye. People in a rush often forget to acknowledge the service or favor one is receiving. When was the last time you thanked the person who bags your groceries? Have you thanked someone who helped you learn something in a class lately? What about a health-care provider who stitched up a bad cut or treated you for the flu? Has someone corrected you when you were in the wrong?

The helpful things others do for us should be acknowledged. Don't forget to give a genuine smile along with your thanks.

THOSE WHOM WE FEAR

Let us consider fear. All animals face danger. We are equipped with a sense of fear to protect ourselves from injury. In the wild, the young are born with instinctual reactions to the unknown. We humans are born with reflexes, where our bodies automatically react. Unlike other animals, we don't begin to actually *fear* things until our brain has developed for about a year. This is when we become frightened of separation, strangers, and other things we aren't used to. This is also the time when lifelong fears of people unlike us can be instilled.

In your notebook, make a column with the heading, "Age." Next to it, make a column titled, "Experience." List the age at which you met people outside of your immediate family under the first column. In the other column, record your reaction. This can be a paragraph or a few words. Go through your life, thinking back to each time you ventured or were forced outside of your comfort group. Below the columns, describe in a few sentences how your experiences shape the way you feel about people today. Is there anything you regret or would like to change?

Finally, ask a close friend or relative from a different group, (racial, cultural, religious, sexual orientation...) to do the same exercise. Compare your results. Having done this exercise, what have you learned about the source of your own fears, their validity and how to address them?

MELDING

Investigate the genealogical backgrounds of five interesting Americans. These can be politicians, celebrities, historical figures, or your own friends. Traced back a few generations, many families include individuals from other racial groups and cultures. America is not just a melting pot; it is a blacksmith's forge in which all immigrants are tried.

"Through many dangers, toils, and tears we have already come," the hymn states. Becoming accepted is easier for some by virtue of status, money, race, and sex, yet most of us will be tempered, like disparate metals. We are a country of invaders and invaded, the enslaved, the indentured, and the immigrant. The melding together is what follows when our various peoples see the beauty in each other and begin to fall in love. The merging of our strengths is what has always made this country strong.

Look up your own family's background, gathering strength, pride and inspiration from what your ancestors risked and endured to make life better for their descendants.

I HAVE MADE A MISTAKE

Learn the phrase, "Everyone makes mistakes." If you are a person who judges yourself and/or others harshly, think of this phrase before you open your mouth. Ask yourself, "What have I learned from my mistakes?"

In your notebook, list five mistakes you have made, large or small. Analyze what led you to make them. What happened as a result? Re-write the scenario, imagining how you could have avoided the mistake. In order to take responsibility for your error, learn to say, "I made a mistake," rather than, "Mistakes were made," which implies that *someone,* not necessarily you, screwed up.

Now, pick five other people whom you believe to have made mistakes. These can be friends and relations, cultural icons, or politicians. Repeat the same exercise with each.

READYING YOURSELF FOR RESPONSIBILITY

Consider the word "responsibility." When we break it down, it means our ability to respond. When we take on the commitment of raising a living creature, we are obligated to meet their needs, although it means sacrificing our own for quite a while. Most of us in this position make a lot of mistakes and over time, learn to respond much better. Anyone with children knows that all the above applies to little humans.

If you are considering having children, first experience what real childcare is like. Visit people with little kids. Babysit for someone. And most of all, make sure your partner is on the same page as you in terms of responsibility and sacrifice. You might consider developing a list together (based on your research about childcare) of the costs and responsibilities necessary for raising an infant, such as feeding, diaper changing, cuddling, stimulation, and bathing. Break each caring task down into specific details. For example, if the infant will not be breastfed, what is required to obtain and prepare food for the newborn? How much time will be required? Once you and your partner feel your list is fairly complete, it is time to exchange how each feels about sharing the tasks.

Now, repeat this exercise, but this time with a toddler in mind. Your list will include such things as potty training, teaching your child to share with others, and helping your child to develop self-control. This is also where you will list how you feel about daycare. Again, investigate cost ahead of time. Methods of discipline should be on this list, as parents need to be consistent to avoid confusing their child.

You may take this exercise further, with elementary school, middle school, all the way through high school. Have fun with these exercises. The more you know about your partner's philosophy of child-rearing, the smoother your life together will be.

If you find you have extremely different views on important topics, this would be a good time to find a childcare specialist with whom you can talk things over. When you are ready, nothing will compare to (or prepare you for) the wonder of watching and helping a young human to grow into a strong, responsible adult.

TIRED OF WAITIN' FOR YOU

The next time you have an appointment with someone, and they keep you waiting, note the following:

1. How long did you wait?

2. Did they or their assistant inform you of the delay?

3. Was the place in which you waited comfortable?

4. When the person showed up, did they explain their delay?

5. Did they apologize?

6. How did you feel about this later?

Certain people are always late, by an hour or more, showing up without an excuse or apology. Ask yourself and your friends if you are guilty of this. If so, schedule things with more time in-between so you can be sure you have a margin for error.

Organize the day before so you won't lose time picking out clothes, looking for your keys, etc. Be sure you have the address of your agreed upon destination, as well as the number of the person you are meeting. If you work in a hospital or are a doctor and things back up, give the patient updates as to the wait. Most people understand delays; lack of consideration is harder to forgive.

A COOL DRINK

On those boiling hot, humid summer days, fill your portable cooler with cans of seltzer and water. Cover with ice so they are nice and cold. Take them to a job site where there are people working in the heat, like a highway crew, a police detail, firemen & women, electrical or telephone line workers. Offer them a cold drink and tell them it's a gesture of appreciation for the job they are doing. Provide a bag for disposal of the cans and let people know you will return to pick them up later on.

NUANCES OF MEANING

Consider the difference between these words: intellectual, intelligent, learned, cunning, and charlatan. In your notebook, list each on a separate line, then write synonyms next to each. Look up each word's definition. On a separate page, write the difference between the words. For example, how is the word intelligent different from the word learned? When is an individual a charlatan; when are they simply cunning? A person may be cunning, yet still not be a charlatan. These differences are important to understand if we do not wish to be fooled.

Americans, throughout our history, have sometimes been tricked by charlatans in our government, our media and our daily lives. Being intelligent and informed should be a goal for everyone. Even a smart person, if uninformed, can be tricked by cunning individuals into making bad decisions.

The word intellectual has become a pejorative among certain groups who have redefined it to mean an elitist snob. When we allow others to define words for us, we lose our ability to communicate effectively with each other. From time to time, look up the definitions of words and phrases you hear frequently used by people with access to a platform.

Words are links in the chain of communication, which is essential for healthy relationships between people.

ADAPTATIONS

One of the reasons we humans have been a fairly successful species is our ability to adapt. According to the U.S. Census Bureau, in 1800, roughly, 97 percent of our country was rural; by 1990, 75 percent had become urban. Despite the tremendous difficulties and upheaval this transition caused, people adapted.

We are, however, better at adapting to certain problems than we are at fixing them. Predicting how change will affect our culture is *not* one of humanity's greatest strengths. Humans leap before looking to see where we will land.

Americans have adapted to having weapons of war on our streets. We shrug off cruel, rude, or incendiary remarks by some of our elected public officials and hurry past fellow Americans living on the sidewalks. Not all adaptations are bad ones, however. In your notebook, make a list of five times Americans have adapted to things which improved the quality of our lives. Spend some time considering how those adaptations continue to benefit us. Now, think of five instances where our adaptations were to the detriment of humanity or the planet.

Finally, identify at least five situations in which Americans pushed back and refused to adapt to a bad idea. In your personal life, are there adaptations you have made that you would like to change? Choose one and develop a plan to improve your situation. Act thoughtfully, but act!

LA LA LAND

If you are totally stressed by the world and feel as though you are about to burn out, take a movie break. Pick two or three movies at a multiplex and spend the day gorging on them, one after the other. Take a stretch break, buy lunch, sit in the lobby in-between films, but do not leave the theater. Choose stories, fantasies, or animations. Avoid movies that will wear you out with explosions, catastrophes, or real-life tragedies.

The idea is to remove oneself from the world for a day immersing yourself in a place where your mind won't ruminate over your problems. You will emerge rested and ready to resume your life, having taken this break.

A GROWING TREE

Choose a tree; one you see nearly every day. This will be your teaching tree. Spend some time observing it from far away. In your notebook, describe the shape, color, size, and the way the texture appears from afar. Now go to the tree and observe the same things, close up. Touch the bark. How does it feel? What shape are the leaves? Do the roots protrude above ground? How old would you guess it to be? Find out what species of tree it is.

Every day at the same time, look at your tree and note any changes. It may seem as if the tree stays the same, but nothing stays the same from one moment to the next. You must be very observant. At some point, you will notice a change in its colors, especially if you live in a Northern climate. Find out some things about your tree's needs online. Is the tree healthy? What kind of life does it sustain? Observe the things others fail to notice. You will learn a great deal about life. When we turn our interest and attention outward, we cease to obsess about our inner worries.

ARE YOU LISTENING?

Decide the next time someone tells you they have a problem that rather than immediately giving them advice, you will keep still for a while until you are sure they have no more to say. Then ask, "How does that make you feel?" This gives the person a chance to examine their feelings and work out the problem. It also gives you, the listener, a way of actively listening, rather than thinking of the next thing you are going to say.

PART OF THE SOLUTION

Call reputable charities whose background you have checked and ask them to send you promotional material or hand-outs for their organization, such as collection boxes, buttons, or stickers and an official letter stating that you are collecting money for them. Get a group of teenagers involved, with parental permission. Have a meeting where everyone proposes ideas about how to raise funds and pick one or a few of the ideas.

Much of the world is suffering from famine, climate disasters, war, persecution, and disease. Young people who feel helpless to do anything to improve things or have an effect upon their world become anxious and depressed. In past eras, adults and their families often worked together, as farmers, or manufacturers. Each member of the family contributed. Even the smallest of children helped gather food, feed the animals, or work in the family business. These days each age group has a separate culture. We need the energy and hope of the young *plus* the experience of the old.

The Boomers had a saying, "If you're not part of the solution, you're part of the problem." Working with our kids, our grandkids and everybody else's kids creates ties, understanding and is a lot of fun for everyone.

IN READINESS

Prepare yourself for emergencies. Do you have a place to go should something happen to your house, apartment, town, or area? Plan with friends and relatives to take each other in if necessary. Be sure everyone in your family knows where to go should you get separated.

Next, do your best to put away some money for a disaster. Remember that if bank machines are down, you may not be able to obtain cash in an emergency. Make sure you have gallons of water stored, along with canned foods and a can opener. Having a variety of canned meats, fish, vegetables, and fruit that you like is essential. You can always use the cans you feel have been stored too long, replacing them with new ones.

You should also have a stockpile of medical supplies, including prescription drugs and personal products like soap, tampons, razors, and toilet paper. It doesn't hurt to have a change of clothes, as well. Don't forget your pet's requirements, food, medicine and bowls, leashes and nail-clippers.

Hopefully, you will never experience a disaster, but being prepared means being able to sustain oneself and one's family, should it become necessary. It also provides us with peace of mind.

IRON HORSE

High summer can be stressful for those with no ability to cool down. If your apartment or house is too hot, take a break. Find out what it costs to take a train ride. You may have to find a way to get to the train station if you live in the country. Buy a round-trip ticket for someplace that requires at least an hour ride each way. You don't need a particular destination: the journey itself is the whole point.

Pack a basket lunch with plenty of snacks and fruit and something to drink. Bring your pen and journal or tablet. Get a window seat and go early so you can observe commuters. Describe the people as they get on the train. Eavesdrop on conversations and note them down. Talk to the people next to you once they've settled in if they seem amiable (unless they're trying to read). Ask them where they're going and tell them what you're doing. Then, turn your attention to the scenes outside your window. What does America look like from your perspective? Record your thoughts about what you see and how it makes you feel.

If your ride is a long one, take a nap. When the conductor isn't busy, tell him/her what you are doing. If they have a dialogue with you, ask them about themselves and what it's like working as a conductor. People enjoy sharing stories about their work with someone genuinely interested.

If you don't have access to a train, but are near the water, take a trip by boat. For example, every summer when the New York City heat becomes unbearable, you might take a ride back and forth on the Staten Island Ferry. Wherever you live, there is some form of public transport which will take you on an adventure. If you are far out in the country, it may take some planning. It will be worth it. Refresh yourself!

AN ANCIENT BIRD

Go online or, if possible, to a pond or lake where you can see and hear wild loons. An ancient species, loons have a serpentine grace. They spend most of their lives in the water, fresh water in the summer, saltwater in the winter. Their legs are set further back on their bodies than most other waterfowl, so they have great trouble moving about on land. Their heavy bones allow their bodies to ride just below the surface of the water. They are not highfliers and must run across the surface of the water some distance to take off.

Loons, however, are agile as seals once underwater and can stay under for long periods. They carry their babies on their backs. When mature, during mating season, loons in the northeast have black heads, necks and beaks, white breasts, and finely patterned black and white feathers on their backs and wings. Their eyes are red, like rubies. They have an unearthly cry which echoes off the mountains surrounding their watery abodes: the very voice of nature. They have been on earth longer than humans.

Look up Loons on the Internet and find out all you can about them. You might enjoy doing this with your family. If you have children, once you have read everything together, ask them to draw a loon. Make a loon sock puppet and have it tell a story. Learning about the other animals who share our environment is a grounding experience for those periods when we are feeling sad and alone.

OBJECT OF DESIRE

Are you a happy person? What makes you happy? Make a list of ten things that make you happy in order of degree: number one being the happiest. Find friends or relatives and ask them to compile a similar list. Compare your lists.

Note the types of things you have listed. Are they things that we take for granted until we lose them, such as good health, friends, or people who love us? Are they experiences, such as traveling, doing hobbies, or dining out? Are you happiest when you acquire objects you desire?

Now, write next to each thing you've listed, why this makes you happy. Finally, estimate how long happiness lasts when you achieve the things on your list. Share your insights with your group and compare your thoughts.

PLANETS, STARS AND AIRS OF SPACE

Have you ever wished upon a star? Take a trip to your nearest planetarium. Bring along some interested friends. Purchase a star chart while you're there or get one online. On a clear night, go to a place where you can see an expanse of sky without a lot of light pollution. If you live in a city, you could go with your group to a park in a safe location.

Pack a blanket, binoculars and a flashlight. Have your star chart accessible. Locate the North Star and the constellations that appear in your area at that time of year. Once you have identified planets and stars, lie down on the blanket and be still for at least five minutes. Watch the sky. Is anything moving? Do you see any meteors? Lastly, have each person adopt a star; one they can repeatedly locate but as yet know little about. Have each person make a silent wish.

When you return home, find out as much as you can about your wishing star. Is it really a star, or is it something else? Does it still exist out there, or are we seeing the light of something that vanished long ago? Remember that every atom in you was once part of a star and that we are all made from the same materials.

GOOD VIBRATIONS

Play some of your favorite upbeat music and dance. Make sure you are in an area where you won't trip over anything. You may do this alone or with others. If you are unstable on your feet or use a wheelchair or walker, then dance while seated. Make sure you use your legs and your arms. If you live with a toddler, do this exercise with them. They will teach you some good moves you may have forgotten.

Dancing is a great aerobic workout. The music makes the time pass quickly and you are more likely to repeat an exercise if you enjoy doing it. Vary the types of music you play. This is your opportunity to ask friends whose culture is different from yours to bring their music and come dance with you. If you form a group of interested people, you may even choreograph a dance.

Talk to your local exercise facility about using a space to meet. Aerobic workouts are often employed in treating depression. Elevating one's heart rate supplies the brain with more blood, which can improve the brain's functioning ability. Of course, always check with your doctor before beginning any strenuous physical activity and start slowly.

STANDING UP

What do you stand for? For whom do you stand? If your child or another family member was being bullied or abused, would you defend them? If you saw a stranger being picked on, would you come to their aid? If your country was being polarized by lies, would you search for the truth?

If government or conglomerate businesses should damage the environment for their own profit to the detriment of all living things, would you speak out? Make a list of the things you stand for, in order of importance. Choose one issue about which you will thoroughly inform yourself.

Then volunteer to help your chosen cause. Standing up for what you believe means you will be less likely to fall for everything.

YOU ARE NOT ALONE

When we are frightened by illness, whether the fear comes from actually having a disease or fearing that we will catch it, those worries may separate us from others. We feel trapped inside a glass jar. Looking out, pressing our faces against the glass, we perceive the world going on around us, seemingly without a care. This is a distortion.

At some time, most of us will experience feeling cut off from happiness and health. At those times, we need to realize that all of those happy people are just like us. Eventually, we will again be outside of the glass. Even when we are far apart, we can keep in touch using the phone, the computer, or with cards and letters. Making contact with isolated individuals is the greatest kindness. Listen if they want to relate how they feel. Ask them to tell you a story about their life; about a time when things were going well. Help them relive their joyful memories. Watch their favorite happy movie with them. Call their friends and relatives and ask them to visit.

People can face all kinds of things if they are not alone. In the olden days, we had our families around us for support when we were ill and isolated. You can be the person who helps lift that glass jar and gives the person trapped within a breath of fresh air.

WEIGHTLESS

Let us find a way to float. We begin our existence floating in a vast dark sea of nutrients. The moment we are born, gravity begins to hold us down so that we forget what it is like to be suspended in a liquid. Some of us are lucky to have access to the ocean, a lake, river, pond or pool. These are great places to float if you know how to swim. Bring a friend along for safety.

If you have no access to water, or are not a swimmer, consider purchasing a child's wading pool. Make sure it is long enough to lie in. If you wish, you can float atop a blow-up water mat. Fill your pool with at least four to five inches of water. Pick a sunny, windless day. Lie on your back in the water or on your floatation device and let each one of your muscles relax.

Think of yourself as floating through the air. Imagine your body's weight evaporating upwards, so that all that is left is a gossamer skin filled with helium. Close your eyes. Know that you are floating on the surface of our blue-green planet. Breathe easily and deeply. Lie there as long as you can and then rise refreshed.

SWIMMING.

Fig. 8.—FLOATING.

TACT AT FAMILY GATHERINGS

Call someone in your family with whom you share mutual respect. Ask them if they might be willing to discuss the political differences among family members. The idea is to identify possible problems before they occur. If you will be attending important family gatherings, especially during the holidays, it can be helpful to make a plan to deal with philosophical and political differences that may arise.

There might be, for example, family members who will insist on glorifying or disparaging public figures. Ask the organizer of the gathering to establish a few ground rules. Family members could collaborate on these ground rules over email ahead of the event which would garner more buy-in. For example, people might agree not to discuss politics at the family gathering, especially if there is alcohol involved. Should anyone slip and begin an argument, someone could say, "I am interested in your point of view about this. Let's make a date to get together and talk it over."

THINGS WE PUT AWAY

Take out your notebooks and describe ten experiences you enjoyed during childhood that you miss. Do the same for the following periods: ages thirteen through eighteen, eighteen through
twenty-five, twenty-five through thirty-five, and as many decades
after this as you have lived. Spend a lot of time thinking about
each period. Consider what it was about each event that made you
appreciate and recall it.

Once you have completed this, look over what you have written.
Most likely you will see a pattern that will tell you a little bit about
yourself. Try to summarize what you once experienced in a few
words, such as "I laughed a lot," or, "I loved playing on a team."
Now, choose one of the things you listed and work on bringing it
back into your life. You will need a plan, perhaps advice as well.
You must think outside the box because you are in the habit of
doing without whatever it was that you once experienced and lost.
Find a new way back to those things you loved about yourself and
your life.

EAT OUT

Plan a picnic for someone who needs one. Do you know someone in your family or at work or in your community who is going through a really rough time and could use a respite? Get some others on board and go buy a large cooler, big enough to hold food, beverages, plastic plates, knives, forks, and spoons. Buy some cloth napkins and a tablecloth as well. Check for special diets or food allergies, buy a small, cooked chicken or prepare some vegetarian or vegan dishes. Wrap them up in foil. Now find some yummy side dishes, like deviled eggs, pickles, both sweet and sour, a nice baguette or loaf of Italian bread, and several cheeses. Make or buy a cake. Be sure you pack some fruit too. If the person enjoys wine, a nice cold bottle of Rosé or a white wine is perfect for summer. If not, lemonade, ice-tea, a festive bottle of non-alcoholic grape juice or seltzer can be added. Buy some plastic glasses to include and don't forget to pack an opener.

Choose a nice day and location. Most areas have parks (with access to bathrooms) or places open to the public. Arrange your transportation. You and your friends who are hosting the picnic should also provide a blanket and some folding chairs if needed. Often, the people who most need a picnic will not arrange one as they may be too worn out. You will all profit from being in the fresh air and enjoying a good meal together.

WATCH YOUR STEP

The word, "Footwork" was used to describe a style of music and dance that originated in Chicago in the '90s. The word is used, as well, to describe movements in most types of dance and sports. Let us consider our own everyday footwork. There is an old expression that goes, "Watch your step!" This is a warning to people about to "step over the line."

There are times when stepping over the line can cause injury to us or others. How many of you walk, or, far worse, drive with your attention focused on your iPhone? Any player of sports will tell you that footwork needs to be practiced before it becomes effective, yet most of us devote no time to thinking about where and how we move our bodies, much less our feet. Footwork involves mental rehearsal, as well as physical. Consider where and how you walk. What are some of the perils you could encounter by not paying attention? Make a list in your notebook. Check out your house, your office, your car, and your personal habits.

Where are the inherent accidents-about-to-happen? Now, consider the last time you didn't "watch your step." What happened as a result? In dance, music, and athletics, poor footwork yields poor performance. In the wide world, it can cause death and destruction. We all need to think ahead, plan, rehearse, reflect and then move...as well as "watch our steps."

YARD WORK

Is there a home near you that is run-down or where the yard is overgrown and the person who lives there can't tend it? Is the owner alone and depressed, unable to afford help or to do heavy work themselves? Find someone this person trusts. See if they would discreetly ask the person whether they would like some (free) help from folks who live nearby who love to garden for themselves and others.

Get one or two friends to come with you. You may offer to mow, clip overgrown bushes, rake or plant flowers. If the person is able-bodied, they may be lured out of their house by curiosity. Invite them to help, if they can. Sometimes, when we are wounded, we withdraw into cages of our own making. Once someone else cares enough to open the door, it is easier to step outside once again.

TO THE LAST DROP

Involve your family in saving water. Many of us take for granted the fact that when we turn on the faucet, water comes out. In many places, droughts have rendered the land dry and barren. In others, available water is tainted with lead, and heavy metals or is simply bad tasting.

We fortunate ones often let the water run while we wash dishes or brush our teeth. We shower longer than necessary. Take note of your habits. Within your household, have a plan for your water use. Make a bet as to who in your family conserves water the best over a period of days and give that person a prize. Only when we are conscious of our habits can we amend them.

AN ACKNOWLEDGEMENT

Write a note or letter to a person close to you. Explain why you appreciate and love them. Mail them the note.

ANONYMOUS FAMILY

Each time you go to the grocer, garage, drug store, school, hospital, or anywhere you frequent, look around at the people who work there. Find out their names if you don't already know them. Pay special attention to positive things that they do for you and the public in the course of their jobs.

Bring a little pad or record notes on your phone every time you visit. The fact that they show up early or stay late or work on weekends can be part of your list of their virtues. Look around; be descriptive. Are these people patient, and friendly with cranky customers? Do they look you in the eye and smile at you?

Once you have collected enough information, write one of those holiday letters people write at the end of year, describing the accomplishments of their children, vacations, and any losses or gains to the family. Your holiday letter will be about the people you have been studying, and their attributes, instead of your own family. Brag about their accomplishments and good qualities the way one does about one's own blood relatives. Then send the letter to the manager, director, or owner of the establishment. Write it out by hand on pretty paper. For some folks, the people with whom they work *are* their family.

SAFE?

A health professional who notices a particularly bad bruise on their patient's arm asks how it got there. He or she is right in asking. Many of us know people who have been battered, either as children or as adults. This is a "dirty little secret" people are reluctant to reveal.

Domestic assaults go on all around us. We, as a society that accepts far too much violence, have lots to do to fix this problem, including prevention, counseling, better laws protecting victims, and, most important, educating ourselves and others on the subject. If you think someone you know is being battered, explain that you are concerned.

Find out what professional help is available in your town. If there is no adequate service, organize a community meeting to talk about establishing a program. Your health care provider may give you some tips. Note: Men can be victims too and are even *more* reluctant to admit they are being battered for fear of being shamed.

Having a stable community requires that we watch out for one another. No one should have to deal with being beaten or emotionally bullied.

FOOD SECURITY

Fresh peaches, warm from the sun, apricots, tart and juicy, tomatoes harvested from a real outdoor garden, blue-green kale, chock full of iron and nutrients, crisp apples plucked from the tree, tender lettuces, corn harvested that morning to be served hot, dripping with butter; the very flavor of summer! We take for granted that these things will be available, along with fruits and vegetables from other parts of the country shipped fresh to our markets.

But what if there is no market within a drivable distance? If you lack transportation, are elderly, physically challenged, or have small children, going long distances for food is impossible. Do you live in an area where stores selling fresh produce have moved to safer locations? Farmer's markets have sprung up in many cities and affluent suburbs. Visit the nearest one and speak with the vendors. Ask how far they will go to sell their produce and whether they would support having a market in your area.

Gather your friends and neighbors to form a committee to help make this happen. After creating a plan that includes suggestions for possible locations, times and dates for your community's farmer's market, contact your town or city's leaders and request a meeting. Permits need to be issued, the location chosen, and health and safety problems discussed, including security, refuse collection, and parking permits for the vendors. Start small, with a few vendors. Eventually people from the community might obtain their own stalls to sell crafts and baked goods. Find out the possibility of organizing a trip to one of the vendor's farms with the neighborhood kids and their parents. Get their school involved. Healthy food leads to a healthy society.

A TOKEN

Go to a flea market or swap meet and look for someone who sells old coins. Sometimes you will find old European, Asian, Canadian or South American coins that are of little value to collectors. Buy a bunch of these, take them home and clean them up with metal polish; never mind what you heard on Antiques Roadshow! Look up each coin's country of origin.

Take them with you to give to kids you know, kids with unrealized potential. (Make sure it's ok with their folks first). Sit down with the young person and say, "This is a very old coin from_____ (filling in the country's name). Thousands of hands have touched this coin before it has come to you. I want you to take it and think of the stories of some of its previous owners. Imagine a story in which someone just like you worked hard to achieve their dreams. Keep the coin safe and whenever you are tempted to give up, hold that coin and think about the person in your story. Then try again. When you do succeed, which you eventually will, pass the coin on to someone else and tell them just what I've told you. No, it's not a magic coin...you don't need magic because you have all you need to succeed within you. The coin is just a reminder."

A THERAPEUTIC TOUCH

Offer someone you are close to a back rub. Have them lie down on the floor on several blankets so that their head is slightly lower than their body. Warm their back with a heating pad or warm towels for a few minutes to loosen up tight muscles. Then using a little massage oil or olive oil which you have warmed in your hands, work into the muscles.

Do not rub hard over bony areas. Work your way down the spine on both sides to the muscles of the lower back. These are often tight and tense from daily stress. Tightest of all are the shoulder/neck area muscles. We hunch over our devices, putting unnatural stress on these muscles.

Ask for feedback from the person you are massaging; "Can I push harder? Does this hurt?" There are many online tutorials for learning massage. Sometimes, just having the touch of another person can be therapeutic.

THE CONCEPT OF TIME

Find a few eight-year-old children you can interview with their parent's permission. Ask them the following questions: "Can you tell me what the word 'time' means? Are all times the same?" Then ask, "Why does the time you get to spend having fun (for example, playing with your friend) seem shorter than the same amount of time doing something you dislike (for example, doing homework)?" Write down their answers in your notebook.

Now, ask five fifteen-year-olds the same questions, recording their answers. Repeat this exercise with five thirty-year-olds, five sixty-year-olds, and five people over the age of eighty. Compare the answers people give at different stages of their lives. Have you noticed any similarities? How do you account for them? Lastly, ask yourself what activities make time seem to pass quickly for you. When you are becoming bored or depressed, choose to do one of those activities.

TREE RUBBINGS

Take a pad of white drawing paper to the woods, or someplace where there are trees. You will also need a dark crayon or a stick of chalk with the paper removed. You will be doing rubbings of tree bark. Take a page out of your book and hold it against the tree. Now, using your crayon's side, *lightly* rub it back and forth over an area of about 3 inches by 3 inches, being careful not to puncture the paper.

Once you have established a definite pattern that looks like a drawing of the bark under the paper, move on to another type of tree. See how many types of trees you can collect. If each tree is in leaf, pick a leaf, lay it on a flat surface and do the same rubbing of the leaf.

Go home and try to identify your artwork by looking up the trees and foliage in your area. If so inspired, use your rubbings as inspiration for a design. The more we know about our environment and the other living things within it, the more we will care about them.

BRINGING UP BABY

Anyone with a small child knows little kids are adorable…mostly. As young creatures, they are exploring the world as well as negotiating their place in it. It is important, as well, for growing minds to learn boundaries and the consequences for ignoring them. This requires that we, as adults, establish rules and adhere to them, such as looking at but not grabbing things off grocery shelves. Wise parents carry toys with them to distract the youngster.

Yet certain parents expect people to ignore the disruptive behavior of their child, viewing those who comment as intolerant child-haters. Everyone expects and tolerates occasional outbursts from youngsters and commiserates with those dealing with cranky or tired kids.

But parents who allow their children to disrupt performances, pitch tantrums in places such as religious services, concerts or non-family style restaurants without removing them from the area create a hostile attitude towards children in public. Receiving attention, positive or negative, teaches a child that *they* are in control, ensuring repetition of the behavior.

Taking the youngster to a quiet place where they are not getting attention for their negative behavior comes first. A parent can speak to them gently but firmly, helping their child to gain control. Fortunately, most people prepare for raising children, learning from family members and friends. We take all manner of tests before we are allowed to drive, get jobs, and pass inspections. Shaping lives, *especially* our own children's, is hard, important work. Take parenting courses and talk to other parents if you are ready

to raise a family. We want our kids to be happy, healthy participants in society. They are the future of America.

A SPONSORSHIP

If you belong to a group of workers, friends, acquaintances, or associations, propose sponsoring a child or family through one of the excellent agencies that are out in the world working with the millions of displaced persons. Divided amongst your group, a monthly payment would cost each person very little, yet make a world of difference to a living, breathing human.

You will be able to communicate with your child and will get progress reports from your sponsoring agency. Knowing you are helping save a life will make you realize how powerful an individual can be when we join together to improve things.

PERSONAL BUOYANCY

Hold a cork underwater and then release it. Notice that the deeper down you hold it, the higher it pops up when released. Keep this in mind when you are in trouble.

If you feel you have hit bottom, remember that cork and refuse to be held down.

COMPASSION AND EMPATHY

Remove your clothes in front of a full-length mirror when you are in private. Look at your body in a non-critical way. Turn slowly, perhaps with a hand mirror, to see your back. Take note of where the body is most protected from the environment. What parts are the coldest? What is the warmest? With a pointed but non-sharp object like a broom straw or a bobby pin, gently poke your body on your arm, belly and calf. Which parts of your body are the most and the least sensitive?

Go into the bathroom, run some cold water and step into it. How long does it take for you to feel chilled? Now make the water warm. Experience the pleasure your body feels as it becomes warm again. When you have dried off and dressed, consider that under each person's clothing is a body like yours, with the same vulnerabilities to heat and cold.

Remember your own body when you read the news about displaced populations. Recall what you have felt when you see someone sleeping in the street and speak out. Becoming active helping our fellow humans draws us out of ourselves, replacing apathy, self-absorption and anxiety with purpose.

WASHED IN MOONLIGHT

Take a moon bath. Plan to go somewhere private and safe on the next full moon when the weather is warm enough and where you can see the sky clearly. Bring a small bowl, a flashlight, a bottle of water, a clean washcloth, a pillow or towel, and a blanket you can roll up and strap below your backpack. Include bug spray and tick repellent.

Choose a shadowless spot where you have a full view of the moon. Spread out your blanket with your pillow or rolled-up towel at the head. Lay down your pack and fill the bowl with water. Place it where you can see the moon's reflection in the water. Put the washcloth next to it. Now, sit down and stretch your arms up towards the moon, spreading your fingers and inhaling deeply. When you feel good and stretched out, exhale and lie down gently on your blanket.

Dip part of the washcloth into the moon's reflection and wash your face with it. Next, wash your neck and arms. If you are wearing shorts or a skirt, wash your legs, re-dipping the cloth into the water often. Remove your shoes and wash your feet. When you are finished, pour the moon-water out onto the grass. Lie down. Stretch your limbs in the moonlight, feeling the coolness of the moon-water as it evaporates from your skin. Imagine that you are absorbing the luminosity and reflecting it back to its source. Breathe comfortably. When you are ready, pack everything back up and return to your life cleansed.

ESSENTIALLY SOOTHING

Go to a health food store and buy a small jar of lavender oil. This is an essential oil and should come in a small dark glass vial. Before you go to sleep, dab a tiny bit on your pillow. (Test a drop overnight dabbed on your wrist first, to make sure your body isn't allergic). Do the same for your family members if they wish. It will help you sleep and relax. If you suffer from excessive worry, concentrate on the fragrance of the flowers. Picture yourself walking through a sunny field filled with lavender. Imagine the sun on your face, birdsong in the air, butterflies of all colors flitting through the blossoms. Do not allow yourself to stew over problems in the last hour before going to bed.

OUTDOORS INSIDE

Collect the first signs of fall for someone who can't go outside. If you live in an area where the leaves are bursting with color, collect the best, brightest samples you can. If you plan to take them into a hospital, you might press them in heavy books until they are dry and flat. Then tape them into a scrapbook which can be easily carried. You can also dry leaves, flowers, and herbs in silica gel, a salt-like substance available online or in craft stores.

Take your camera with you as you search for fall foliage and get photos of the area in which you are collecting things. If you are doing this for a frail or hospitalized adult, they may appreciate photos of areas that are special to them. Kids will love photos of animals. Should you live in a part of the country where the leaves don't turn colors, you can look for other seasonal changes. The desert in the fall is different from the desert in spring. Cities, too, look different seasonally.

Birds typically pass through most areas at certain times. Can you find feathers to include in your scrapbook? If you collect things like nuts, seeds, cattails, shells, or anything bulky, you can keep them in a treasure box where they can be felt or smelled. Small packets of earth, sand, or moss can be added as well. If you can make a video on your phone as you make your way, collecting your samples, the recipient can hear the crunch of your feet on the gravel or the passing noises of cars, bikes, and other people. Being separated from the world is depressing and unhealthy for most of us. You can bring the earth inside for someone.

RIDDLE ME THIS

In the olden days, people entertained themselves as best they could. Often, this involved word games, such as riddles. *Merriam-Webster's* dictionary defines riddle as: "a mystifying, misleading or puzzling question posed as a problem to be solved or guessed." In our world today, we face many issues which fit that definition. Unlike our ancestors, who honed their minds by playing such games, we have lost vocabulary, become less fluent and more reliant upon computers and technology to solve conundrums.

Look up riddles from various eras. Gather some family members or friends and ask each person to come up with several riddles to share. Hint: Children's books used to be full of them in the 18th and 19th centuries. Have a riddle party where each person puts the riddles they've made up into a bowl. Everyone, in turn, gets to pick a riddle to solve.

TAKE IT SLOWLY

Be patient with people who stop dead in doorways, hallways, and supermarket isles, blocking your way. Sometimes, they cannot hear you and don't notice they are obstructing traffic. Smile and gently touch their arm and say, "Excuse me," when they look at you. If *you* happen to be someone who inadvertently blocks the way, try to be aware of your body in relation to its surroundings. If you need to stop walking in a crowded place, move towards the wall so you are not in danger of getting knocked over or obstructing others.

Pay attention to the people nearby, especially if your sight or hearing has diminished. All of us need to watch out for each other, especially for people with balance issues, making sure we don't rush or push them.

DREAM COME TRUE

Imagine something wonderful; something you would love to see realized during your lifetime. This can be something you would like to change about your own life, such as attaining a skill you never dared to try. It could be something you would love to have happen in your own town or community. Maybe you are envisioning fulfilling a dream for someone else. Or perhaps you would like to make something that will last long after you have gone. Whatever you decide on, take out your journal and start brainstorming.

Write down everything about this dream. Make a list of all things required to attain your dream. Pick one of these things and break it down into small steps: what would it take to do this? Keep breaking things into smaller pieces until you can actually make one of them happen. In this manner, climb your way, piece by piece towards your goal. If you can imagine it, you have a good chance of attaining it.

APPRECIATION

Collect small pieces of paper for each person who will be a guest at a family gathering. On one side of the paper, write the name of each guest. Now fold the paper into a small square so that the name is hidden. After dinner, while people are still gathered at the table, pass around a small bag containing the folded paper squares and have each person take one.

Go around the table in turn, with each person saying something they like about the person whose name they picked.

A LIFE PLAN

When we are young, a year seems like an eternity. During child-bearing years, we lose track of time, looking forward to the next weekend's escape or vacation. But around retirement, we begin to look back at our lives, marveling at how fast time has passed.

We regret having not attempted certain things. Regardless of your age, take out your notebook and make a life plan. If you have kids of school age, you can do this with them, as well. First, write down your talents, intellectual strengths, and interests. Now list features of your personality, for example, you are obsessed with detail, you don't like being told what to do, or you are a natural leader. Next, list the things that interest you, such as participating in sports, inventing things, cooking, studying science, participating in politics, creating music, art, or working with people. Lastly, brainstorm how you can, based on what you have written, find out more about your field of interest. Visit people in fields you'd like to explore. If you have teenagers, this is an especially valuable exercise for them. If you are retired, you already have had an extraordinary number of experiences and know a wide range of people.

Now, why not plan your next decade? You'll never know how far you can travel if you don't keep walking.

TRACES OF LIFE

Let us examine the tracks of other animals. You will need a notebook of unlined paper, a drawing pencil or a number 2 pencil, and an eraser. If you have a camera, bring it along. Find an area that animals are likely to visit. This can be woods, a marsh, a vacant lot in a city, a desert, or a park. Most animals prefer areas not frequented by humans (rats and other scavengers excepted).

Look around until you find some interesting tracks. Take a photo or try to draw the track. Does the animal have claws? Does it hop? How big are the tracks? Take notes, including where you found the tracks. Now examine some domestic animal tracks: dogs and cats, birds if you live in a city; cows, horses, sheep, chickens, snakes, lizards if you live in the country. You can usually find Canadian geese tracks everywhere these days. Some areas boast wild turkeys, coyotes, raccoons, possums, moose, cougars and bears. If you are really ambitious and near a zoo, you may be able to study more exotic tracks. Once you obtain a collection of tracks, look up the ones you can't identify, especially those native to your area. Find out why animals have developed the type of feet they have. Once you have learned about our fellow animal's footprints, consider the kind of footprint humans leave on our shared planet.

TOGETHERNESS

Celebrate with others whenever you can. It's a great way to make friends. During the 1950s, many people joined bowling leagues. The leagues were like clubs for adults to get together. It was common for bowling leagues to hold family picnics and parties where everyone pitched in and made food. The kids spent the day running and playing while the parents drank beer and soda and sat around laughing. It didn't cost much, but everyone had a great time with their whole family together.

These days, many towns and cities provide free events where strangers can meet each other. Art openings, block parties, concerts, and parades are places to gather. With people tied to their electronic devices, it is tempting to try to get things done, rather than taking time to be with friends, family, or strangers. We're always in these little boxes; cars, homes, office cubicles, which separate us from others. As a result, many of us are lonely and depressed. If you find yourself alone too often, seek out what is available in your area. Take a risk and go. You have nothing to lose and may gain a whole new world!

FROM MY HANDS TO YOURS

Start the Warm Hands, Warm Hearts project. Go online or to a material store and buy some patterns for mittens and hand warmers; the kind you sew from old sweaters or fleece material. Be sure you get several sizes of patterns so you can make them for men, women, and children.

Put an ad in your local paper and flyers around your town stating that you are looking for people who can sew; people of all ages, to fashion warm gloves, mittens, and hand warmers for people who have lost everything. Ask for donations from the public for the purchase of supplies. Find a place like your library, Senior Center, or a local craft shop that will let you hold your gatherings. Tell everyone to bring sewing scissors and any clean old wool clothes or sweaters they don't want. Ask several people with portable sewing machines to bring them along, too. Look up the various disaster relief agencies that are helping people. Call and tell them what you'd like to donate, making sure they will have a way to distribute what you make. Once you have your contact established, determine any supplies you will need that you may need to buy (fleece, thread, etc.). Contact the manager of fabric shops in your area and see if they will help. When all is in place, schedule several sessions and get started. Make sure people bring some refreshments. Ask young people to participate. Find experienced knitters and sewers to give knitting and crochet lessons on-site. The goal is to have boxes full of warm mittens that have been hand-made to donate. Ask each crafter to write a little note to include encouraging the recipient of their gloves.

THE COMFORT OF YOUR COMPANY

When, in your travels, you find yourself in a room along with other people peacefully pursuing an activity, whether or not these people are strangers, friends, or family, take it in. Look at the faces of the people.

Do they look content, stressed, happy, or exhausted? How are they seated? Are their bodies slouched or sitting formally? What is the atmosphere like? Is it busy, with people leaving and arriving constantly, as people on a break, or are people settled in to read, work, or do whatever it is they are doing, quietly, as in a library?

How does being here at this moment with these people make you feel? Now, keeping in mind the chaotic world in the news, look around you again and be grateful for the quiet and comfort you have at that moment.

YOU'RE THE TOPS

Documentary filmmaker Ken Burns once said that we humans are hard-wired for war. "We didn't get to be the top species by being nice," he stated. Let us explore what being a top species entails.

In your notebook, title a page: Qualities of a Top Species, and list what you imagine them to be. On the next page write: Qualities of a Bottom Species. Again, decide what those qualities are. Now, examine the two lists. Ask yourself if you agree that we are a top species. Are there any humans who do not seem to be hard-wired for war? Are there other species that are as successful in their own right as humans? Would you describe them as war-like?

Now, make your own list of the qualities you would *like* a top species to possess. Do you think humans can develop those qualities? What changes would that require in our thinking? Consider how you, personally, can help those changes to occur.

THE THRILL OF THE HUNT

Prepare a treasure hunt. This can be for a birthday, anniversary, graduation, or any time you want to please someone in a special way. There are several ways you can go about this: Your treasure can be small items that delight, hidden in various places, or one big treasure. The idea is to provide either a treasure map or clues which lead a person to the next hidden clue or treasure.

Artists amongst you might draw a map. Look up historic treasure maps for some examples. These are usually aerial views of the grounds to be searched. You can draw some topography, visual clues, footprints, arrows; whatever makes it fun and interesting. If you plan to actually bury a treasure, the map will end with an X or, perhaps a sign saying, "Dig Here!" If your treasure hunt is to be indoors, give the hunter the first clue card. This can be a small poem or a riddle that points the way to the hiding place of the next clue. For example, "If you're patient and you're kind, behind this door a clue you'll find."

This is fun for people of all ages and adds to the anticipation and pleasure of receiving the gift.

UNIQUE

Buy, find, or make a drawstring satchel to hold small stones. Spend some time searching for what strikes you as the perfect stone. The stone might be round and smooth. Or it might be jagged and oddly shaped. You may feel drawn to a stone that is a single eye-catching color, like a deep green or maybe marbled.

Take the stone home, wash it, and keep it in your satchel. Carry your satchel with you to go stone searching again another day. Try to find an *identical* stone and keep looking until you think you have found one.

When you bring it home, examine both stones with a magnifying glass. Take notes on your observations.

DISCOURSE

Americans are fascinated with British royalty, assuming our own society is classless. Yet, we have the expressions, "working class," "blue collar" and "white collar." Americans are hard workers; many holding down two or three jobs to get by. Very few of us don't need to work. Like the Brits, Americans tend to socialize with those we were raised with.

Archie and Edith Bunker would have little opportunity to get to know a family living on Park Avenue. While we think of our culture as egalitarian, we tend to form relationships with those having similar educational opportunities and jobs. As stratification increases, our understanding of each other decreases, resulting in a lack of empathy.

The unscrupulous amongst us can more easily turn one group against another for their own gain. This rising level of mistrust, violence and social inequality can only be addressed if we are willing to speak with each other. Find someone who may have a different life situation from yours. This could be someone you see every day, but never have a real conversation with. Ask them what they think about the weather. Say something like, "When I was a kid, the weather was very different. It seems like we have a lot more storms now." Then sit back and listen to what the person has to say. Even if you disagree with their opinion, pay attention, nodding to show that you are listening. If there is time, you may go further and ask, "Why do you think that is?" This is a good conversation opener.

Regardless of one's economic, financial or educational background, we all have opinions about the weather. The idea is to reach out to someone from a higher or lower economic strata of society than yours. The person may be surprised that you asked. Perhaps this will open a door towards further conversations. Don't argue with the person; you're not challenging their point of view. You're just having a dialogue.

If we really want to form "a more perfect union" we must first be aware of each other's feelings. You can be the start of that.

TUMBLING AFTER

When was the last time you rolled downhill? Are you fortunate enough to live near a grassy park? Does it have gently rolling hills? Find one that doesn't have any poison ivy or rocks and lie down at the top of it. Now, close your eyes and stretch your arms straight out above your head.

Let gravity take over as you begin your roll. Enjoy the smell of the smell of the grass. Note: You may end up slightly green, so wear old clothes. This is best done barefooted.

TO PRESERVE OR DEPLETE

Consider the words, "save" and "spend." They are antonyms in one usage. Saving usually has a positive connotation. We save money, when we can, for leaner times. We save lives, sending food, medical care and money when natural disasters strike. We save time, regarding time-saving devices as good.

When we spend money, it can be in a positive or negative way, depending upon our motivations. All of us spend our lives, whether we want to or not, just existing. Everyone spends time in ways they regard as pleasing or not. Take your notebook out and write on one page heading the word, "spend." List at least ten ways you are spending your life. After each, write a little commentary as to whether you want to change what you're doing and spend your life on something else?

On the next page, write the word, "save." List ten ways or things that you save and comment on each. Are you saving things that are meaningful to you? Finally, examine the news with an eye to what the world regards as worth saving and spending.

AMERICA, STILL BEAUTIFUL

The American news media increasingly highlights more bad news than good because the bad draws more attention. As a result, many people, including adolescents and young children are developing anxiety disorders. The violence we see on the news, the lack of progress towards equality and fairness, as well as our own social isolation which has increased over the years, has many people in despair about the future of our country.

Your task is to find true stories of lifelines that courageous and kindly Americans have thrown one another. Write the stories down and at the end of each week send one to your local newspaper or radio station. The Pew Research Center reports that when Americans "look toward the not-too-distant future, they see a country that in many respects will be worse than it is today." If the news Americans hear concerns only negative stories, we have no reason to be inspired.

But there is another face of America which still shines with hope, pride, goodness and strength. That face is the face of courageous older citizens, who speak out against ageism or racism which affect all generations of Americans; it's the face of young people, who declare loudly, "What matters is not *whom* we love and chose to spend our lives with, but *that* we love and care for one another."

America's face is the face of fathers of daughters and sons; men who say, "A good man uses his strength to be a steward of the planet, to protect those he loves and those to come." It's the face of women, our sisters and mothers, grandmothers, declaring, "We own our bodies. No one has the right to sell us, beat us or control our fertility." America's face is many-colored, multi-shaded, and shares the same red blood, feels the same cold, hunger, loneliness, shame, pain and pride. America's face has beards, lipstick, braces, tats, wigs, and piercings and is freshly scrubbed.

America's hands are the calloused hands of laborers, and fishermen, the manicured hands of executives, and the small hands of the next generation. America is a land of gay, straight, bi, and trans people. Americans still help each other, laugh together, weep together. Don't let the bad news cause you to despair. Collect and share the good stories occurring every day; and take heart.

CHANGING HORSES

Stop the World, I Want to Get Off! was the title of a Broadway musical. Have you ever stopped your own world and gotten off or changed its course? In life, a person can spend decades learning and practicing an art, a sport, a skill, or working at a job only to realize they are unhappy or unfulfilled.

Starting over is hard, and yet, if you are miserable with what you are doing, consider changing. Each of us has a finite period of time on Earth to live our lives. Some trudge through it day by day in despair, rather than alter course.

You can stop your world and get off, changing horses on your personal merry-go-round. Lay your plans carefully. Talk to lots of people. Do your homework, so that you have a high likelihood of succeeding in your new endeavor. Get help and support. When you are ready and know where you want to land, JUMP!

I SWEAR IT'S NOT TOO LATE

Do you love warm weather? If you live in an area that is known for its variety of seasons, you are probably surprised at the increasing warmth each February. Go outside and enjoy the weather. See if bugs have arrived that usually don't show up until spring. Are there birds in your area that don't belong there yet?

The great folksinger, Pete Seeger, wrote a song, "Turn, Turn. Turn", based on Ecclesiastes, chapter 3 vs.1, which begins, with the words, "To everything, there is a season and a time for every purpose under heaven." Consider this if you like wearing shorts and a T-shirt in New England in February. It's tempting to say how great it is; "It's just like spring!" But it is not spring. Next week it may snow, killing the birds who, confused by the climate upheaval, have arrived early, only to find no available food.

To the other species, there is truly "a time for every purpose," and we humans bear the responsibility for altering that schedule. Enjoy the nice weather, but speak up when people say things like, "I'm all for climate change. I hate the cold." Don't argue, but beg to differ, explaining why. Spend a little time looking up the average temperature in your area over the last few decades.

Arm yourselves with information so that when you are in conversation with others about climate change, you will have scientific data to offer, rather than just your feelings. If your town has a climate action group, attend a few meetings to see what you can do to help the planet, whether it be writing letters to your elected representatives, learning about alternative energy programs or campaigning for candidates who care about the future of the Earth.

GAUGING YOUR SOUNDNESS

Sometimes you will find a burden left at your feet. Try to pick it up, asking for help if you need it. How you handle it will teach you about your strength.

EPILOGUE

I returned to playing my harp, writing songs, telling stories, and making art. My creative non-fiction stories have been published in literary journals. Using my gifts and the skills I have developed over my life have been crucial to staying healthy. Rather than obsessing about problems, I become involved in fixing them. We competed in agility trials with my Border Collie, Liberty. My husband Dan and I continue to perform in public. I'm committed to doing whatever I can to help all of the creatures who inhabit our miraculous planet to live happier, safer lives.

ACKNOWLEDGEMENTS

Thanks to S. Talbot Thayer, for teaching me that all art requires hard work, sacrifice and discipline.

Thanks to all nineteen members of the Roommate Club for having lived with me at various times in all my many manifestations.

For teaching me to be a decent creature, thanks to Rags, Spot, Widget, Noel, Shenandoah, Katie, and Liberty.

Thanks to my parents for caring and providing for me; I know you loved me.

Thanks to the friends who were there for me when I needed them.

Thanks to Bob Strom for his technical assistance with publishing.

Special thanks to the two individuals whose corneas have allowed me to continue seeing. You are forever with me on my journey.

Thanks to Pete Seeger for making me believe that a song can change the world.

My deepest love and thanks to my husband, my greatest critic and admirer, my accompanist, editor, pizza chef, barefoot runner and favorite skeptic.